Understanding the Inter
Student Experience

Universities into the 21st Century

Series Editors: Noel Entwistle and Roger King

Cultures and Change in Higher Education *Paul Trowler*
Global Inequalities and Higher Education *Elaine Unterhalter and Vincent Carpentier (Editors)*
Managing your Academic Career *Wyn Grant with Philippa Sherrington*
Research and Teaching *Angela Brew*
Teaching for Understanding at University *Noel Entwistle*
Teaching Academic Writing in UK Higher Education *Lisa Ganobcsik-Williams (Editor)*
The University in the Global Age *Roger King*
Understanding the International Student Experience *Catherine Montgomery*

Further titles are in preparation

Understanding the International Student Experience

Catherine Montgomery

palgrave
macmillan

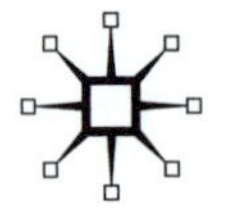

First published 2010 by
PALGRAVE MACMILLAN

Palgrave Macmillan in the UK is an imprint of Macmillan Publishers Limited, registered in England, company number 785998, of Houndmills, Basingstoke, Hampshire RG21 6XS.

Palgrave Macmillan in the US is a division of St Martin's Press LLC, 175 Fifth Avenue, New York, NY 10010.

Palgrave Macmillan is the global academic imprint of the above companies and has companies and representatives throughout the world.

Palgrave® and Macmillan® are registered trademarks in the United States, the United Kingdom, Europe and other countries.

ISBN: 978–1–4039–8619–1 paperback

This book is printed on paper suitable for recycling and made from fully managed and sustained forest sources. Logging, pulping and manufacturing processes are expected to conform to the environmental regulations of the country of origin.

A catalogue record for this book is available from the British Library.

A catalog record for this book is available from the Library of Congress.

10 9 8 7 6 5 4 3 2 1
19 18 17 16 15 14 13 12 11 10

Printed in China

For my mother and father
who taught me to value education. And for Ellie, of course.

Contents

Series Editors' Preface

The series is designed to fill a niche between publications about universities and colleges that focus exclusively on the practical concerns of university teachers, managers or policy makers and those which are written with an academic, research-based audience in mind that provide detailed evidence, argument and conclusions. The books in this series are intended to build upon evidence and conceptual frameworks in discussing issues which are of direct interest to those concerned with universities. The issues in the series will cover a broad range, from the activities of teachers and students to wider developments in policy at local, national and international levels.

The current pressures on academic and administrative staff, and university managers, mean that only rarely can they justify the time needed to read lengthy descriptions of research findings. The aim, therefore, is to produce compact, readable books that in many parts provide a synthesis and overview of the often seemingly disparate issues.

Some of the books, such as the first in the series – *The University in the Global Age* – are deliberatively broad in focus and conceptualization, looking at the system as a whole from an international perspective, and are a collection of integrated chapters, written by specialist authors. In other books, such as *Research and Teaching: Beyond the Divide,* the author looks within universities at a specific issue to examine what constitutes 'best practice' through a lens of available theory and research evidence.

Underpinning arguments, where appropriate, with research-based conceptual analysis makes the book more convincing to an academic audience, while the link to 'good practice and policy' avoids the remoteness that comes from an over-abstract approach. The series will thus appeal not just to those working within Higher Education, but also to a wider audience interested in knowing more about an organization that is attracting increasing government and media attention.

Noel Entwistle
Roger King

Preface

Aims and background to the book

The aim of this book is to enable those working or studying in Higher Education to develop an advanced understanding of the social and academic experience of international students. This will enable them to consider ways of refocusing their approach to working with and interacting with others in an international university context. The book presents a contemporary approach to the experience of international students* and an individualized and personal picture of the international student in Higher Education is offered here, showing these students' experience as the human aspect of forces of internationalization. The book explores their social and cultural context and its impact on their learning experience in Higher Education.

International students are transient visitors to our academic communities, yet they form an integral part of the social, cultural and academic context of Higher Education in the UK, Australia, New Zealand, the United States and other countries. Although individually these students remain in universities for a limited period of time, as a group they are always present on campuses and in classrooms and are therefore a significant element of the social and cultural landscape of Higher Education.

The increases in the numbers of international students travelling from their home countries to study in Higher Education abroad have brought the issue of the effects of their presence on campus and in class to the forefront of discussions in educational research and policy. Much has been written and published on the subject of international students'

* When this book uses the term 'international student' it refers to students who have travelled from their home countries to study in Higher Education in another country (Carroll and Ryan, 2005). This group consists of students who are normally resident outside the host country, and in the case of the UK this would include students from the European Union, who are considered 'home' students for fees purposes but who may share experiences with students from more distant shores. The book also refers to home students, meaning students who have chosen to go to university in the country where they have previously been educated; in the case of the research that supports this book these students are from or resident in the UK (ibid.). The final chapter of this book, however, questions the use of these terms.

role in Higher Education across a number of national contexts, in the UK (Carroll and Ryan, 2005; Kinnell, 1990; Furnham, 1997), in Europe (Teichler, 2004), in Australia (Stone, 2006a), in New Zealand (Ho, Holmes and Cooper, 2004) and in the United States (Lee and Rice, 2007).

The rise in numbers of international students has initiated discussion of some new and key topics in universities' teaching and learning missions and quality enhancement groups, with calls for urgent work to be done in promoting and valuing diversity. Institutional and national surveys have been initiated and universities across the globe are asking how best they can support these students and develop international student support systems both in central university departments and within Schools and Faculties.

An implicit perception of international students is that they choose to remain in their own nationality groups and have difficulty in becoming involved in social exchange with other students who do not share their 'culture' and language. This picture of a group of students who are isolated and disadvantaged by their lack of contact with 'British culture' is questioned by this book. The main research project underpinning this book presents an alternative view of international students and their experience of studying in Higher Education. This view, based on research, shows an individualized picture of an international student group who are benefiting from the effects of internationalization of Higher Education possibly more than their home student counterparts. The main research described in the book focuses on a contextualized, wider view of learning at university, emphasizing that learning and development in HE is much more than simply what goes on in the classroom, and is embedded in an influential social and cultural context.

This book concentrates on research in the field of international student issues, and, in addition to presenting a critical review of current research in this area for staff and students who may not have the time to research the topic in this depth, it also describes one research project in detail. It is envisaged that this book will be of interest to a wide range of staff who work within the Higher Educational context; to those who are teaching international students or who are researching the student experience or intending to begin research or evaluation in this area.

The university context is now made up of a diverse student body that includes rising percentages of international students. It is hoped that the consideration of the social networks of international students will raise awareness of the importance of these relationships to the international learning experience and inform the practice and research of those working and studying in an internationalized university context. As Beard, Clegg and Smith note 'We need richer conceptions of students as affective and embodied selves…it is important to understand the lifeworld of students' (2007: 235).

An outline of the research supporting the book

The central chapters of this book are based around a research study that looked at the social networks of international students and reflected on the influence of their social networks on their learning experience. The study explored aspects of a group of international students' experience of social contact and focused on their relationships both in their academic activity and in the environment that surrounded the classroom.

The project data was collected over a six-month period in 2004 in a UK university and thus represent a snapshot of a group of international students at a particular time and place. However, it is hoped that the issues and experiences of this group of students will have resonances with other groups of international students in contexts beyond this time and geographic situation.

The primary aim of this study was to consider social factors as part of the learning environment and to look at the relationship international students have with their social and learning environment. Throughout the study, and throughout this book, the significance of learning beyond the classroom is emphasized. Learning takes a great number of shapes and forms and often takes place in contexts beyond the classroom and beyond university walls. This implies a view of education that goes beyond acquisition of the academic degree or how students acquire subject knowledge. Rather, this study has a focus upon the personal and social experience that students have during their time at university.

The study employed a qualitative methodology, using semi-structured interviews and an extensive shadowing scheme where students were followed on campus to classes and tutorials and in their everyday life at university. This was done in order to access a rich picture of experience, presenting the university context from the perspective of the students themselves. The shadowing of the students became a very significant part of the study, and spending extended periods of time with the students on campus informed the findings of the project to a large extent. The research sample was a purposive one and focused upon a selected social group of international students.

As far as choice of student in this study is concerned, students who were established in their studies were selected to avoid the focus on 'settling in' or 'adjustment' which often dominates studies of international students (Altbach, 1991; Beaver and Tuck, 1998; Furnham, 1997; Unterhalter and Green, 1997). A form of snowball sampling was used to select students who were part of a loose social network, beginning with two students who were friends and selecting other students who were known to them. This involved seven students from six different nationalities: Chinese, Indonesian, Nepalese, Indian, Dutch and Italian. It was decided to choose the students across nationality, relying on a social network rather than the politically constructed divisions of nationality. The study consisted of data drawn from two exploratory focus groups, a pilot study involving four students and a main phase with seven students. The analysis and pinpointing of themes were data-driven, developing a coding system where themes emerged and were recorded through use of a computer database.

As with much qualitative research, the data of this study is in-depth but is drawn from a relatively small group of students. There is no claim here that this group of students are 'representative' of the international student community, but, in similar contexts, issues and aspects of experience of this student group could be resonant with other international social networks. Readers of this book will be able to note where the international student group they are familiar with is similar or different from the group presented here. To this end, further contextual data is provided in chapter 3.

The methodology of the research that supports this book follows a constructivist approach. This assumes that what is 'real' is jointly constructed by individuals and groups and that there are multiple, often conflicting constructions of reality, but all of these are meaningful (Schwandt, 1994). This is not to say that it is impossible to establish any kind of 'truth', but, as Schwandt puts it, a constructivist view considers that:

> truth is a matter of the best-informed and most sophisticated construction on which there is consensus at a given time. (1994: 128)

Thus this approach maintains that an individual's experiences are 'authentic' or valid in their own right and the individual's perspective forms the 'truth' of an event. This is the view which underpins the perceptions presented in this research.

The choice of this approach relates back to the fact that the research of this book focuses upon seeing the experience of international students from their own perspective. Here we consider the learning experience of international students, and so it is important that this experience is presented from their perspective and is viewed as being embedded in its social context. More details of the methodological approach of the study are presented in appendix 1.

It is also important to note that the constructivist approach acknowledges that researchers and theorists are also themselves immersed in the context in which they are researching (Strauss and Corbin, 1994), and so are participants in their own research. Because of this, a reflective account of the researcher is provided in appendix 2 of this book.

An overview of issues raised in the book

This book is divided into three sections:

- Background and context
- The main research study
- A discussion of the ways forward

The initial chapters will consider crucial background issues, and central chapters of this book will provide an insight into the findings of a research project about the social networks of international students. The final section is made up of a chapter that discusses ways of thinking about international education in the 21st century.

The first chapter of this book will consider the culture and discourse surrounding international students in Higher Education. The idea of culture is one that is used when talking about international students, and the phrase 'it's a cultural thing' is often used to explain difficulties in interaction or international students' approaches to study. Culture is often cited as the concept that illuminates the differences in diverse student groups, but it is a concept that is rarely interrogated. Thus, the issue of 'culture' and its bearing on learning will be discussed here. Spencer-Oatey (2000) views culture as an explanatory concept and notes that when faced with someone who is of another nationality we immediately note difference. The idea of culture may then be used to avoid considering in detail why someone may behave in the way that they do and, more importantly, why we ourselves behave in the way that we do.

Ideas relating to culture may lead to stereotypes being applied to the social and learning experiences of international students. Some of these stereotypes relate to learning and some relate to social interaction. With this in mind, the importance of empirical research that systematically tells the stories of international students cannot be overemphasized. Individual stories of international students are crucial to developing a positive image that counteracts a deficit model that may sometimes be applied to international students.

Familiarity with empirical research that individualizes international students as learners in Higher Education may contribute to the breaking down of stereotypes. Because of this, chapter 2 of this book will consider some key research that relates to international students. This chapter will provide a wider context for the main research project of this book by considering research that has been carried out about international students in Higher Education in a range of countries. Research that spans three decades and large-scale quantitative research will provide an important contrast to the qualitative in-depth approach adopted by the main research project of this book.

Chapter 3 then presents seven vignettes of 'real' international students who took part in the research project around which this book is based. This chapter provides contextualization of the experiences of this group of international students and illustrates the individual nature of their backgrounds and experiences in Higher Education. Understanding the students who provide the voices in the book places their responses in context, enabling the reader to gain a better picture of their experience. Chapter 3 also explains the thinking behind the methodological approach to the study, outlining its distinctive features.

A picture of a strong international student group, part of a strong and supportive network that resembles a community of practice, is shown in chapter 4. This purposeful and highly motivated international community appears to have developed as a means of replacing social capital lost in transition from the international students' home context. It is the suggestion of this book that the development of a strong international network may enable students to acquire lifelong learning competences that could prepare them to live and work in an international context. Engagement with the international student community may be a means of preparing for life and work in an intercultural context. It is suggested here that through their education abroad students are preparing for a future in a community that has an international outlook.

Chapter 5 considers the relationships between international and home students. It is sometimes suggested that international and home students have difficulty in working together and forming profound friendships based around academic exchange at university. The image of international students as an isolated community seeking out their own nationality for support is one that has been quite frequently presented (Spurling, 2006). This book presents detailed research data that shows a more complex picture, with evidence that contrasts with the idea of the culture-centric international student and provides a richer picture of the motivation of home students.

Research suggests that students' motivations for studying abroad relate to their sense of the significance of their education in a global context (Merrick, 2004). The development of language skills, for example, was perceived by the students in the research project supporting this book as a means of learning to live with others and learning about the culture of a new context. English is viewed as an international language that allows students to gain entry into a more global arena. In addition to improved language skills, students also perceived the ability to communicate well with others of different cultural and social backgrounds to be an important skill and one that would be useful in future work and social life in a global context. Chapter 6 of this book aims to show that this global community is one that exists in students' perceptions of their experience and in the students' view of themselves. It is suggested that the idea of a global community is one that is embodied in the international students themselves.

Chapter 7 presents some brief conclusions to the research project on international students' social networks, drawing together some of the issues raised throughout the preceding chapters. The conclusions underline the fact that the international student experience is complex. The tensions between international students being a strong social group yet also retaining their independence, being a group who wish to develop profound relationships with home students yet still retaining some fears and preconceptions about this, emphasize the complexity of the social and cultural context.

The final chapter of this book opens a discussion on ways forward and new ways of thinking about international experiences of Higher Education. The chapter pinpoints the crucial nature of the discourses that we use to describe the participants in an international university context, and problematizes binary terms such as 'international' vs. 'home' and 'East' vs. 'West'. The chapter suggests some ways of thinking about teaching and learning in HE and underlines the importance of the teaching and learning context in influencing intercultural interaction. Finally, the chapter discusses the approach of 'internationalization at home', which shifts focus away from the international student group towards a more inclusive learning community that looks outwards to internationalize itself. Some example case studies of teaching and learning projects that aim to achieve this are then given.

Finally, the book concludes with a postscript written by one of the students who took part in the research study. The purpose of the postscript is to provide a continuation of a story begun here and to further emphasize that this book is about real people who have developed during their experience at university and whose lives have changed in the course of this book being written. In the postscript Isken reflects on his early life before he came to university abroad and talks about what he has done since leaving his undergraduate course. His reflection represents a real example of the significance of the social, cultural and personal background to education and learning abroad.

At the current time in Higher Education, it seems crucial to consider and understand the significance of the social dimension in which learning occurs, as this has implications for ways of thinking and practising in universities. Byram and Feng (2004) acknowledge that more research in the area 'beyond the traditional classroom' is needed. They note that this sort of research focuses on situating language and culture learning in social contexts and they underline the 'value of understanding *processes of culture learning from the perspective of learners in informal contexts*' (Byram and Feng, 2004: 151).

Acknowledgements

I would like to acknowledge the contribution of Liz McDowell and thank her for her continued support and encouragement without which this book and the research project that supports it would not have been possible. I'd also like to thank colleagues who have made comments on the text: Adrian Holliday, Sheila Trahar, Andrew Shipton, Michaela Borg, Kay Sambell, Nicola Reimann, Kerry Harman and Erik Bohemia.

Part 1
The Context

1 Culture in Higher Education

This chapter looks at some aspects of the culture and discourse that provide the context for international students' learning in Higher Education. Here internationalization is recast as a culture and ideas of marketization are presented as an influencing discourse on the experience of international students. Discourse is defined here as choice and use of particular language and how that choice and use carries implicit meaning and values (Richards, Platt and Weber, 1985).Culture is defined in detail later in this chapter but in terming internationalization a culture it is intended that it is seen as a set of beliefs and values that underpin a perspective on Higher Education. The idea of culture itself is one that is seen as significant in the experience of international students, mainly because of variation in national cultures. The aim of this chapter is to present a critical perspective on the idea of culture as a means of encouraging a questioning approach to this issue. Culture is often seen as the explanation for the challenges encountered by students and staff in an international context but the idea of culture itself is rarely interrogated. This chapter will address this by investigating some of the important issues associated with culture and its relevance in Higher Education.

The culture of internationalization in Higher Education

Internationalization is part of the contextual background to the spread of international students in Higher Education across the globe. It is a strong contemporary culture in Higher Education but it is not a new one, as the phenomenon of travelling abroad to study has been a facet of education for centuries, since 'wandering scholars' moved from place to place to broaden their learning (Bruch and Barty, 1998: 18). Publications on the internationalization of Higher Education can be traced back to the Middle Ages and up to the end of the 18th Century (de Wit, 2002; Fok, 2007).

The contemporary internationalization of Higher Education is part of a wider set of global forces, all of which have accelerated the growth in international student numbers. New technologies and new political orders have initiated a process of 'global change' whereby national and social borders have undergone reassessments (Belcher, 1995: 5). There is a new global competitiveness and a struggle for global economic power between giant trading blocs such as North America, Europe and South East Asia (Belcher, 1995: 5; Scott, 1998: 127). It is mainly between these wealthy trading blocs that travel for Higher Education has become possible and more commonplace.

Internationalization in education is a process which has been set in motion by globalization and describes what is happening at a national level, namely that national institutions of Higher Education are reaching out to other national institutions in order to reflect new commercial and political order. Internationalization has implications for academic disciplines (Trouillot, 2003) and has influenced their thinking and theorizing as well as the structure and content of courses in Higher Education. The effect of these complex global processes is global student mobility on a larger scale than has been possible before.

As with the concept of culture, definitions of internationalization vary according to context and perspective and there is considerable variation in the meanings attributed to the term (Knight, 1997; Gunn, 2005; Fok, 2007). Stone (2006) notes that the question of what internationalization means 'invites seduction into a quagmire of potentially unsatisfying responses' (2006: 334). The concept itself remains elusive and although resources, programmes and institutions of many countries across the globe are 'mobilised around the concept of internationalization' a clear and comprehensive definition of the core idea is still 'conceptually elusive' (Callan, 1998: 44).

A common perception of internationalization in Higher Education is that it is the integration of an international or intercultural dimension into the teaching and research of an institution (Deardorff, 2006; Wachter, 1999; Knight, 1995). Many sources also agree that the introduction of this intercultural dimension is seen as a means of increasing the quality of the institution and the education it provides. De Wit (1999) adds the term 'intercultural' to his definition and also stipulates that internationalization includes both international and local elements.

Knight and de Wit (1997) note that there is no simple concept of internationalization but that it is a multitude of aspects that aim to promote an environment that actually integrates a global perspective into the whole university. From the point of view of benefiting the student learning experience, internationalization should not just be viewed as a matter of building collaborative links with institutions in other countries and bringing large numbers of international students to the home institution. It is a matter of internationalizing the outlook of staff and students, both international and at home, and also of internationalizing the attitudes of people in the wider community of the university.

The perception of the nature of internationalization can be determined by the stakeholders who are involved in the process, and the goals, rationale, resources and individual institution will determine the way that internationalization is pursued (Kishun, 1998: 64). Stone (2006) points out that, instead of asking what internationalization means, universities should be asking 'why internationalise' and 'what *should* internationalisation mean?' (2006: 334).

It also appears that commitment to internationalization rests on a 'relatively fragile foundation' and there is a perception that the philosophies and principles of internationalization have not spread to all areas of Higher Education institutions (Callan, 1998: 45). Indeed in 2007 Edwards notes that, as far as internationalization is concerned, she feels we are 'still having the same conversation we were all having in the 1970s' (2007: 373). This may be an indication that some institutions may have developed effective recruitment policies and support systems but are not extending the intercultural dimensions mentioned above into the teaching, support and research cultures of the university. Thus the experience of some students, both international and home, may remain untouched by the potential benefits of internationalization.

The discourse of 'marketization' in Higher Education

Dixon notes that universities are being 'forced into the market place in ways that are reshaping them in their purposes and in the knowledge they create and disseminate' (2006: 320). International students are part of this 'reshaping' process. Universities now rely on the income from the fees of international students and have therefore developed complex marketing strategies to bring international students to the UK, Australia, the United States or other countries. There is competition between universities both across the globe and within countries to attract international students. Institutions have developed a powerful interest in retaining international students and have therefore set up robust student support networks within universities.

As a result of universities being market-driven, the views, wants and needs of students are now being seen as much more significant. In some quarters students are now looked upon as 'customers' with all the legal rights of a 'consumer' because they pay for their own education in a much more direct manner than before. The introduction of fees for home students in the UK appears to have spread this perception to a wider spectrum of the student body. As competition between universities within countries becomes stronger, the significance of student 'satisfaction' surveys becomes more crucial and responding to the views of students is now seen as highly significant. Many universities in the UK and in other countries are becoming much more responsive to the requests and views of their students, particularly their international students, who are their highest-paying 'customers'. These words attached to students are part of the discourse of marketization that circulates in contemporary Higher Education.

This view of Higher Education as a commercial business that operates with a 'customer service' philosophy represents a discourse that may have changed society's perception of the meaning and purpose of Higher Education. In turn this may have influenced both the motivation of students and their experience of that education (Mann, 2001; Dixon, 2006). International students are viewed as part of the commercial aspect of universities, and at times this overshadows discussion of their personal, social and individual purposes in pursuing study at university abroad.

Further underlining the prominence of the marketization discourse surrounding international students, some of the research that has been carried out relating to international students has been motivated directly or indirectly by a move to improve recruitment (Pelletier, 2003). This confusion between research about international student issues and market research driven by recruitment agendas has at times muddied the issues in this area. Pelletier notes that this type of market research, ironically often carried out by international students themselves, has dominated the research carried out in the field. This focus has perhaps limited the sorts of questions that have been asked about international students' experiences and produced little emphasis on more theoretical ideas or longitudinal research (ibid). Teichler (2004) states that:

> It is surprising to note how much the debate on global phenomena in Higher Education suddenly focuses on marketisation,

> competition and management in HE. Other terms such as knowledge society, global village, global understanding or global learning are hardly taken into consideration (2004: 23).

It appears that the impact of the marketization discourse is also having an influence on moves to internationalize the curriculum of Higher Education (Caruana, 2006). Understandings and misunderstandings of the relationship between globalization, internationalization and the development of the global 'knowledge economy and learning society' are driving approaches to curriculum in conflicting directions, according to Caruana (2006: 23).

Despite this there is a consensus emerging that universities need to refocus their efforts on enabling graduates to develop skills that may help them to function effectively in an international world of work (ibid).

Culture and international students

Because of the diversity in national cultures represented by international students, the idea of national or ethnic culture is one that is closely associated with their experience. This discussion of culture attempts to disassociate the idea of nationality from culture and suggests ideas other than culture that could be more usefully applied to international groups.

First, however, it is important to carefully consider the complexity of the concept of culture so that we can understand how its continued use can influence the experience of the international student in Higher Education.

What is culture?

'Believing that man is an animal suspended in webs of significance he himself has spun, I take culture to be those webs' (Geertz, 1973: 5). The concept of culture is a highly complex one and is bound up in many different disciplines and aspects of thought. Williams (1983) notes that culture is one of the two or three most complex words of the English Language. He suggests that this is partly because of its 'intricate historical development' but also because it has come to be used in several distinct intellectual disciplines and in some 'distinct and incompatible systems of thought' (1983: 87).

The complexity of the concept of culture is a maelstrom in terms of considering international students and in some ways it can be misleading and rather unhelpful. Smith notes that culture is an elusive concept that is both 'slippery' and 'chaotic'. He also notes that culture can signify a great deal when it is clearly and coherently defined or can mean little, particularly if it is simply seen as being synonymous with everything 'social' (Smith, 2000: 4).

Laying aside the definitions of culture that relate to Art, Music and Literature or what is sometimes known as 'high culture' (Smith, 2000: 4), culture is also viewed through the observable behaviour of an individual or group, for example through what the group eats or wears in certain countries. In addition to this, leisure habits, marriage traditions and so on are seen to be symbolic of a community's culture. However, at times these local practices can be associated with individual personal characteristics, and this is when cultural stereotypes can develop.

A more in-depth view of culture would indicate that it is not just observable behaviour but a system of symbols and meanings that are underpinned by rules, meanings and beliefs that are not always obvious or observable (Oxford and Anderson, 1995). The metaphor of the 'cultural iceberg' also suggests that there are many aspects of culture, indeed the majority of its aspects, which are subconscious and invisible, lying below the waterline. Beliefs, perceptions and values, against the more obvious aspects such as clothes and certain behaviour, all make up a complex picture of a concept that is as difficult to observe as it is to define (ibid.). Having said this, there are also key aspects of culture that are observable and recordable, such as language, and which provide profound insights into the culture of the individual and the group.

Definitions of culture indicate that it is structured and learned, and that it changes and develops as groups interact with each other, this change being to some extent a conscious one (Kroeber and Kluckhorn, 1952). Culture is also defined as 'situated cognition', which entwines it with activity, setting or context. In this sense culture cannot be detached from learning and indeed culture and context become part of a learning process (Lave and Wenger, 1991). So, from this point of view, the activities and influences of culture cannot be separated from what is learned or known (Oxford and Anderson, 1995).

Culture is seen as knowledge but also as a cognitive model used to perceive and interpret the world around us. Learning culture is similar to learning a language, and, just as language defines our ability to understand and explain what we observe, so culture is a means of framing both propositional ('know-that' types of statements) and procedural ('know-how' statements) knowledge of that which surrounds us (Duranti, 1997).

Questioning the idea of culture

It is useful to question the idea of culture, as this helps us to rethink some of our ideas about international students. For example the idea of 'the West' and 'the East' is one that orientates some of our ideas about international students. If the cultural concept of the 'West' is questioned it begins to become apparent that this term changes over time and also according to who is using it.

Trouillot notes that the 'West' is not a geographical place but a 'fiction, an exercise in global legitimation' (2003: 1). In addition to its not actually being located in the West but rather in the North Atlantic, the idea of the 'West' has a central focus which shifts to include, or more importantly exclude, certain nations. The 'West' can mean America and/or Central Europe and may or may not include Eastern Europe or Latin America. More recently Japan has been included as a 'Western' nation, not necessarily because of any shared value system but perhaps for socio-economic reasons.

Trouillot (2003) notes that the idea of the West is a 'default category' that works only when it is considered in opposition to an 'East', and there is the implication of superiority versus inferiority in these terms (Holliday, 2007a). In other words, the term 'West' is more a means of excluding other nations or peoples from an imagined global value system than it is a means of unifying them. So the term 'the West' is bound up politically with the ideas of explaining behaviours and also with blame and at times it promotes precisely the kind of racist attitudes which it intends to dispel. Trouillot points out:

> The word culture today is irretrievably tainted both by the politics of identity and the politics of blame – including the racialization of behaviour it was meant to avoid (2003: 97).

So culture could be seen as a term that can dismiss the diversity inherent in communities, and it could be said that the idea of culture is tainted by a history of cultural imperialism, dividing communities into categories that imply inferiority to some and superiority to others. More recently the idea of culture has been questioned as a reductionist notion that essentializes social and historical complexities to simple characterizations that hide social contradictions that are inherent across communities (Duranti, 1997).

It is also the case that many aspects of culture are associated with such a depth of colonial, intellectual and military power and supremacy on the part of the Western world that the idea cannot be used 'without assuming a series of naïve and misleading dichotomies such as "us" and "them", "civilised" and "primitive", "rational" and "irrational", "literate" and "illiterate" and so on' (Duranti, 1997: 23). This emphasizes the notion of culture as blame and the idea that culture has been used as a term which 'explains behaviour away' and serves in some contexts as 'an impressionistic explanation for understanding differences and difficulties in multi-ethnic societies' (Roberts and Sarangi, 1993: 97).

So the idea of culture may encourage a perspective through which difference is emphasized and where individuals assume that culture is something that others have, the idea of culture thus separating communities and groups. Culture may also be used as an explanation for why minority or marginalized groups do not 'merge into the mainstream of society' (Duranti, 1997: 23).

International students could be viewed as a marginalized group, and the idea that culture is used as an explanatory concept in terms of the international student is important to the perspective that this book is attempting to present. An example of this is a story told by an international student participant in the research that supports this book. Pei, a female Chinese student, talks about an angry encounter her friend had with a fellow student. The short extract illustrates the complexity of perceptions of culture, and the sensitivities that can be uncovered. It also illustrates how culture can be used as an explanation for difficulties in intercultural interaction. Pei says:

> For example there are some students from Africa, South Africa, and one time my friends and I sat beside them and one of my friends asked the guy a question about the country or something like that. She said she heard someone said that in Africa people are very poor. And when the guy heard this it was obvious that he was unhappy and we didn't understand why he was unhappy. And she thinks he might be angry. Yeah she just wanted to know if it is true or not because she heard it from others but we don't know why the guy was angry. Maybe it was culture. Yeah [laughs] yeah and next time she is very careful.

To some extent Pei may be justified in thinking that this interactive difficulty has something to do with the concept of culture. The African student may have been offended by Pei's friend's stereotype of his continent being dominated only by poverty and famine. Pei's friend did not appear to see this and would be discouraged in future from talking to this student and perhaps students of other nationalities. She may continue to think that this was because of the African student's 'culture', not her friend's clumsiness in stereotyping his background.

The idea of culture is a highly complex one, and where the term is used qualification and explanation are necessary. Despite this, the term culture appears also to be endlessly fascinating, and the idea has been involved in many aspects of research and has itself been the centre of much research in recent times (Spencer-Oatey, 2000). Further to the above discussion as to the fluid and dynamic nature of the idea, Trouillot acknowledges that it is a necessary concept and says that:

> something akin to the culture-concept remains necessary not only to anthropology as a discipline, but also to social science in general (2003: 97).

Duranti supports Trouillot in the acceptance of the necessity of the term and warns also against the dangers of avoiding definitions of culture, as this process is one that can aid understanding of both similarities and differences in the way varied communities construct their identities (Duranti, 1997).

So the purpose of questioning the idea of culture is to raise awareness of the role of the idea of culture in the continuation of marginalization of minority groups. However, as further sections of this chapter will note, there may be more helpful ways of viewing the idea of culture, and these preferred perspectives may help to dispel some of the negative associations of culture outlined above.

Nationality and culture

There are many stereotypes relating to nationality which suggest a causal link between certain behaviours and particular nationalities. These stereotypes infer that our nationality can somehow influence the way that we behave and that there is a general pattern of behaviour that can be associated with particular nationalities. Baumann (1996) notes that:

> The dominant discourse [relating to culture] relies on equating community, culture and ethnic identity, and its protagonists can easily reduce anybody's behaviour to a symptom of this equation (1996: 1).

Baumann writes that even in academic literature this 'ethnic reductionism' is prevalent, and where 'Asian' informants are quoted he states that their views are regularly interpreted as a consequence of their 'Asianness' (ibid.).

Before examining the perceived relationship between nationality and cultural behaviour, it is important to note the work of Geert Hofstede (1984). According to Holliday (2007a), the work of Hofstede has strongly influenced continued associations between cultural behaviour and nationality. The Dutch sociologist Hofstede carried out an extensive empirical survey of more than 100,000 IBM employees across 40 different nations. The questionnaire asked about respondents' attitudes to personal goals, such as earnings, freedom, cooperation. From this each nation was given a 'culture score' based on the average of responses to the item by the people of each particular nation.

Hofstede then came up with four dimensions of cultural variance, which were: power distance; individualism; uncertainty avoidance; and masculinity (Bond, Zegerac and Spencer-Oatey, 2000: 51). Through this extensive research process the 40 nations were then given a value profile, with scores out of 100 for each of the four dimensions of culture. To give an example, Hong Kong scored high on power distance, suggesting that there is a strong adherence to hierarchical relationships in that society. Hong Kong also scored low on individualism, suggesting a collectivist culture, and low on uncertainty avoidance, which suggests a high tolerance for situations with unpredictable outcomes. Finally it was shown as being moderate on masculinity, suggesting that there is not a high ethos of 'masculine values', emphasizing strength and competition for example, in that society.

Hofstede's work was critically acclaimed when it first emerged and given accolades particularly for the fact that its research was extensive and exhaustive and the book *Culture's Consequences* became one of the most widely quoted texts in the Social Sciences (Bond et al., 2000). However, in more recent years there has been considerable reaction to Hofstede's research on the grounds that, despite its quantitative empirical nature, it simply encourages stereotyping and labelling (Holliday, 2007a).

To look at an example of culture scores carefully, that given for Chinese participants in the study was grouped with the other nationalities of Hong Kong, Taiwan and Singapore. Obviously, the diversity in culture inherent in people of these different nationalities could be immense. Also, other subsequent studies which have repeated the research have come up with quite different results for the same nationalities. Bond et al. ask the question:

> How then can the Social Scientist talk about Chinese culture as if it were a unified reality? At least with respect to values there is no

> one Chinese culture. Surely we need to define the 'Chineseness' of Chinese cultures using different constructs like, say, beliefs, or confine ourselves to thinking about particular Chinese cultures (2000: 52).

Holliday (2007a) terms Hofstede's conclusions a 'seductive positivism' which attracts support through the 'scientific' tightness of the approach he employed. Holliday also goes on to point out that Hofstede reduces national culture to an 'essentialist category which is the major determinant of cultural difference, and the major, rational means for organising, explaining, predicting and testing social phenomena' (2007a: 3). According to Holliday, finding information that confirms these reductionist categories is then all too easy.

So it is important to note the misleading nature of the relationship between a nation and culture. This mistaken direct correlation between nation and cultural or personal attributes and even value systems may lie at the root of many of the broad stereotypes that can lead to misunderstanding across groups and individuals. Nations incorporate a wide range of cultural beliefs and linguistic variations, and this means that treating a nation as one culture is misleading and can promote prejudice and from there inequality.

A nation or country is, after all, in most cases the construct of politics rather than a reflection of a group's value system. Holliday writes that links between nationality and culture have been used from the nineteenth century through to the Thatcher and Reagan governments as a means of furthering the principles of nationalism and the particular purposes of governments. Holliday says that national labels such as 'Japan' and 'Japanese' are a 'social imaginary' constructed though the building of certain discourses (Holliday, 1999: 243).

So, on reflection, it is strange to equate cultural behaviour with artificially constructed groups. It would be more useful to construct communities' behaviours through other parameters such as language, for example, to indicate variation in culture both within and across nations (Bond et al., 2000). Indeed, language is a possible indicator of shared values and shared ways of perceiving and making sense of the world, although the wide range of speakers of a wide range of varieties of English also represent a great deal of cultural diversity (Bonvillain, 2003).

It can be seen that, even after extensive empirical work as in the case of Hofstede's study, culture remains difficult to capture, and conclusions drawn from such research are prone to descending into the realms of stereotype and essentialism (Holliday, 2007a). Approaches to teaching international students should take account of this, and awareness of the precarious nature of conclusions relating to the attributes of whole nation states based upon the opinions and comments of individuals should be noted.

A nation is not a culture and variations within nation states can be as wide as across them. It cannot be said that one or more persons are representative of their nations or even of their cultural group. The socially constructed link between nationality and culture is as potentially harmful in the sphere of Higher Education as it is in politics, and it is one of the principles of this book that belief in these links should be dispelled if a positive internationalized education is to be achieved.

What are stereotypes?

Cultural stereotypes are based in over-generalizations of 'the describer's imagination of an inferior other rather than with objective information about what the people being described are actually like' (Holliday, 2007b: 1). Social psychological theory suggests that a person's orientation to others is governed by individual perceptions of convergence and divergence, that is, whether a person feels that they (and indeed the person they are interacting with) are striving for greater or lesser distance and distinctiveness from themselves (Ylanne-McEwen and Coupland, 2000: 194).

So speakers may make assumptions about the people they are communicating with based on a wide range of contextual and personal factors, including language. A linguistic-pragmatic view of a misunderstanding between people who speak different languages may mean that differences in perception of the convergence or divergence of a group of speakers may well first unsettle the speakers. Second, it may lead to the reinforcement of existing stereotyped expectations of a particular culture. Tanaka, Spencer-Oatey and Cray note:

> Incidents such as these [intercultural misunderstandings] point to possible cultural differences in so-called polite behaviour. If such incidents occur in an intercultural encounter, people may attribute them to 'cultural differences', especially if they offer support for previously held stereotypes (2000: 76).

So stereotypes act as a sort of selective filter through which people view others. Previously held beliefs relating to the culture and values of others are maintained by concentration on aspects of behaviour and interaction which support the stereotype, and evidence that contradicts the stereotype is ignored. Information that supports the stereotype is hoarded and information to the contrary is dismissed.

Holliday states that there is an argument that suggests that stereotypes are practically expedient, that they are 'natural and useful mechanisms for aiding and understanding cultural difference, and that although we know they are over-generalisations they are good starting places' (2007b: 2). The practicality argument is an attractive one for many people, as it suggests that accepting the inevitability of stereotypes can be a first step in replacing them with more accurately positive ones. However, Holliday also notes that stereotypes are insidious and pernicious and can be easily hidden in 'neutral everyday talk' and in 'institutional thinking' (2007b: 3). Once these 'easy repertoires' are established they develop as basic building blocks of understanding that are very difficult to knock down.

Stereotypes and the learning context

In a teaching and learning context students may experience misunderstandings caused by the selective filter that is stereotyping. The learning behaviours of students which support preconceived ideas of learner stereotypes may be concentrated on, and evidence to suggest contradictory behaviours may be sidelined or ignored.

The issue of international students speaking in class and offering answers to lecturers is a case in point; staff may refer to an accepted stereotype of the 'South East Asian learner' as a passive learner who is unwilling to offer spoken contribution to a group. Arguments presented above relating to the diversity represented in a term such as 'South East Asian' show that such a generalization is as unreasonable as saying that 'all students are lazy' or, since 11 September, 'all Muslims are terrorists' (Holliday, 2007a). These are examples of mass overgeneralizations.

The significance of these reflections on the idea of culture and stereotypes is that students' interpretation of the social world around them may affect their interaction with others and perhaps also their development within their education. Stereotypical assumptions about particular student groups could then be considered an influence on the teaching and learning experience.

However, prejudice and stereotype are socially constructed and thus are intensely complex. The construction of group identities and perception of these artificial descriptions of groups involve both the perceivers and the perceived. In some cases stereotypes can be used by the group being labelled as a means of positively constructing their own identities (Francis and Archer, 2005). So the complexity of stereotypes should be acknowledged and the question of their influence should be considered with reference to particular contexts. Within the student body in Higher Education the influence of these views on the learning environment should be neither underestimated nor ignored.

Small cultures and communities of practice: Two helpful paradigms?

It is useful in the last section of this chapter to consider two different perspectives on the idea of culture: first the idea of 'small cultures' as opposed to 'large cultures' and second the idea of the community of practice as a culture. This part of the chapter will consider these two perspectives on culture as a means of recasting the view of culture associated with international students.

If you ask someone about their perception of the idea of culture they will first associate the term with the idea of 'large' entities such as British, American or Asian. Holliday calls for a view of culture that involves two paradigms, large and small cultures, with the idea of large cultures being associated with ethnic, national or international groupings and the idea of small cultures being related to any identifiable or 'cohesive' social group. Holliday suggests that these 'small cultures' should represent a different view of social groupings that does not relate to ethnic or nationality groupings as these reflect an essentialist view of cultures that can easily promote stereotypes. Holliday notes:

> What has become the default notion of 'culture' refers to prescribed ethnic, national and international entities. This *large culture* paradigm is by its nature vulnerable to a culturist reduction of 'foreign' students, teachers and their educational contexts. In contrast a **small culture** paradigm attaches 'culture' to small social groupings or activities wherever there is cohesive behaviour, and thus avoids culturist ethnic, national or international stereotyping (1999: 237).

Holliday applies the idea of small cultures to an educational setting and aligns the idea of how cultures are socially constructed to the idea of socially constructed knowledge. Small cultures can be any type of group that shares activities or cohesive behaviour, and thus these could range from a class group to a more institutional group, such as a university or a hospital. It is important to note that these small cultures are not part of a hierarchical system where they are contained within large cultures or groups. Small cultures are important groupings that are entities in their own right.

This perspective on small cultures as a way of viewing groups in Higher Education is a useful one that could reduce the tendency to stereotype groups of learners. In this way the discourse and perspectives of Higher Education could move away from relying on homogenous group terms such as 'international student' towards more inclusive terms that describe social activity and groupings on a smaller scale. These could also include disciplinary labels or groupings.

The idea of community of practice also views social groups as positive and separate entities that share values and activities. The concept of the community of practice and 'situated' learning are important developments in the educational theory of the 1990s. The idea of the community of practice presents an alternative way of viewing the idea of culture, and supports Holliday's idea of a 'small culture'. Wenger notes that the community of practice is not an exclusively academic notion but one that surrounds us in our everyday lives. Wenger, McDermott and Snyder state that:

> Communities of practice are groups of people who share a concern, a set of problems, or a passion about a topic, and who deepen their knowledge and expertise in this area by interacting on an ongoing basis (2002: 4).

Wenger et al. go further in their definition of the community of practice to describe the supportive and purposeful nature of the group. They describe the relationships between the people of a community of practice as follows:

> These people don't necessarily work together every day, but they meet because they find value in their interactions. As they spend time together they typically share information, insight and advice. They help each other solve problems. They discuss their situations, their aspirations, and their needs. They ponder common issues, explore ideas, and act as sounding boards (2002: 4).

This description of the community of practice is particularly interesting in terms of a learning experience. It has resonance in the idea of a study group that meets to discuss aspects of an academic experience and to support and help each other in the aim of being successful and effective in their learning.

Wenger describes a community of practice as something that surrounds us all in our everyday lives, in our families and at work. He notes that in the example of the family the 'practices, routines, rituals, artefacts, symbols, conventions, stories and histories' (1998: 6) are part of family activity and are what make it a community of practice. Wenger also considers the identity of those involved in a community of practice and also the dimensions of such a group. From this description it appears that a community of practice is in a sense a 'culture', although Wenger does not term it so.

In light of the discussion of the over-complex and sometimes unhelpful nature of the concept of culture, the idea of a community of practice appears a more positive concept than culture because it does not rely on the factor of nationality. There are many senses in which the international student group form a community of practice as they develop a particular group identity that evolves over time as students learn about each other, about their new context and about the nature of Higher Education, and share goals and values. This is discussed further in Chapter 4 of this book.

So it is suggested here that viewing the idea of culture through the paradigms of small cultures and community of practice is a first step towards gaining a new perspective on positive academic and social interaction at university. The small culture view of student groupings would support the development of positive peer support, an important aspect of student learning. This book suggests that the process of social and academic exchange between students of varying backgrounds and cultures is an essential element of a positive and profound learning experience. An alternative approach to developing this could be found through seeing students as belonging to small diverse groupings rather than as 'large' cultural groups that have wide, stereotypical labels and characteristics attached.

2 Research on the International Student Experience: A Cultural Landscape

A wide variety of different topics, methodologies and approaches have characterized research about international students and the research has been carried out over several decades. This varying landscape of thought suggests a breadth of different philosophies about the role of international students in Higher Education. The aim of this chapter is to provide a research context and draw out issues that are crucial to the discussion in this book and in particular significant for the main research project that underpins it. These issues include the friendships and social relationships that provide a context for the learning experience; the 'cultures' of teaching and learning; student approaches to learning; and the influence of language and identity on the learning experience. The research outlined here represents varying perspectives on the student experience. The methodologies include large-scale quantitative projects that contrast and complement the qualitative ethnographically-inflected research of the main project of this book.

The methodological approaches of the research presented in this chapter are significant as they provide information about how the international student experience has been analysed and framed. Much of the research carried out in this field in the 1990s and early 2000s is characterized by larger-scale quantitative survey approaches that aim to investigate the views of larger numbers of students. There have been few studies that have looked at one particular aspect of the international student experience in detail and investigations of the social and cultural context created by the presence of international students are few and far between. Jackson's (2008) ethnographic and reflective narrative of a Hong Kong student is a rare and interesting exception to this. The survey and questionnaire approach to data gathering in this field is in contrast to the main research project of this book, which is a qualitative in-depth investigation of a small number of participants. For this reason it is important to this discussion that the wider picture offered by the large-scale research is included in this chapter, for context and to complement the methodology of the main research project supporting the book.

The aim of this chapter is not to present a comprehensive review of all research relating to international students but to indicate the variety of research that has been carried out in this field, presenting a snapshot of the research that will provide context for what is to come later. The chapter focuses on a selection of research, looking at different national contexts, in particular at the UK, the USA and New Zealand. This choice is intended to provide examples of research from countries that receive large numbers of international students. Some aspects of the research in this chapter have been included to illustrate implicit assumptions of deficit and inferiority relating to international students, and some of these issues were considered in Chapter 1. This chapter takes the ideas discussed there further into the field of education, and, in particular, research on learning styles and approaches to learning and teaching are considered.

Research spanning the years: Social relationships and international students in America

This section of the chapter considers two pieces of research carried out 30 years apart. Both relate to the social relationships of international students and both were carried out in America, a popular destination for international students from around the world. These two studies indicate that similar concerns about international students' social experience have resonated across 30 years but also that thinking in relation to this topic has moved on in that time.

The friendship patterns of international students (1977)

Bochner et al.'s early (1977) research into the friendship patterns of international students stands out as it concentrated on a particular, detailed aspect of the international student experience. Many of the previous studies had been survey-based, resulting in wide-ranging and general findings (Bochner et al., 1977).

The study examined the friendships of 30 international students (from five countries: Japan, Korea, the Philippines, Taiwan and

Thailand) studying at the University of Hawaii and also included a 'comparison' or 'control group' of six American students. The subjects were asked to identify their five 'best friends' and the five people with whom they spent most of their time.

The research aimed to 'predict the intra-cultural and inter-cultural friendship patterns of overseas students ... and to develop a social psychological model of the academic sojourn' (1977: 279). The data was considered against a prediction that students would belong to three separate social networks: (1) a co-national network whose function was to 'affirm and express the culture of origin'; (2) a network with 'host nationals' (Americans in this study) whose function was the 'instrumental facilitation of academic and professional aspirations'; (3) a multinational network whose main function was 'recreational' (1977: 277).

The results of the study appeared to confirm the adherence to the above three social networks and to indicate that the students' strongest network was their co-national network (friends of the same nationality) and thus the most frequent and closest friendships were monocultural. The study also suggested that their second most important friendship group was with home students (Americans) and that the students in the study had a 'substantial number of bi-cultural friendships' (1977: 286). Finally, it was discovered that 'multi-cultural contact was a less frequent occurrence' and it appeared that the relationships amongst different nationalities (excluding Americans) were the least prevalent.

The findings of the 1977 study are interesting, as they appear to contrast with the conclusions drawn in the project that supports this book. In this project carried out in UK Higher Education the bi-national group (i.e. UK 'host' nation and international student) is not a strong social network. Rather, the relationships formed between international students and their UK home student counterparts were of a more superficial nature than the international network. Furthermore, the strong social network in the UK research was the multicultural network, that is, the international, non-UK group.

It may be that the findings of the Bochner et al. study were influenced by the context within which the study took place. The study was conducted at the 'East-West Center' in Honolulu, a part of the University of Hawaii. The aim of that centre was to

> promote better relations between the United States and the nations of Asia and the Pacific through co-operative study, training and research ... and to foster understanding and mutual respect

> among people from differing cultures working together in seeking solutions to common problems. (Bochner et al., 1977: 281)

This ethos underpinning the teaching and research of the context in which the Bochner study took place could perhaps be said to have influenced relationships between students. This is of particular interest as it suggests that, if such an ethos of cooperative study and training is followed, stronger, more positive academic relationships can develop between international and home students. This also underlines the significance and influence of the context in which learning takes place.

International students' perceptions of discrimination (2007)

A more recent study carried out by Lee and Rice (2007) also relates to the social relationships of international students and their 'host' nation (in this case America again). The paper underlines the positive potential of the role of international students in Higher Education, emphasizing the benefits that international students bring to HE and to the wider society. Lee and Rice note that international students bring new perspectives to classroom conversation and increase awareness and appreciation of other countries and cultures. They point out that they also bring knowledge and skills, particularly in science and technologies, and if they remain in the country after their course of study they contribute to the 'intellectual capital' of the host country. Those students who return home may be potential leaders and influential figures of other countries, and thus American or other 'developed' nations' Higher Education institutions will have perhaps played a role in improving relations between countries (Lee and Rice, 2007: 381).

Lee and Rice's research focused on international students' perceptions of experiences of unfairness and discrimination in their social experience in and around Higher Education in America. Their study was initiated against a background of falling enrolments, particularly by postgraduate international students, in the wake of the 11 September 2001 terrorist attack on New York. Their premise was that, in addition to other factors such as tightening visa restrictions and increased competition from other countries, an explanation for the decrease in numbers could relate to an increase in neo-racism and rejection by the home student population and the wider community.

The study involved a survey of 500 students and in-depth qualitative interviews with 24 students from a range of academic fields and a range of nationalities (including India, East Asia, Africa, the Gulf Region and Latin America). The interviews focused on changes in perception of the institution in the US (in a Higher Education institution in the southwest of the US) since enrolment and also focused on personal experiences, particularly instances where students perceived there had been unfairness or discrimination.

Lee and Rice applied a conceptual framework of 'neo-racism' to the social experience of international students, a theory that 'emphasises cultural differences as a basis of discrimination that appeals to popular notions of cultural preservation' (2007: 383). This refers to negative attitudes to other races that are not necessarily based on biological factors such as colour of skin but appeal to 'natural' tendencies to retain group cultural identity. An example of this could be negative attitudes to the way other cultures live their lives, what they eat, how they dress or their use of the 'host' language. This new form of racism does not replace other types of racism. It may be a more sanitized and accepted set of views, but it is discriminatory all the same. Lee and Rice suggest that these types of attitudes can be the root of hostile or negative 'climates' in the educational institutions and communities of which international students are a part.

Their study found that a range of international student 'problems' suggested 'neo-racism' as a cause. Lee and Rice associate difficulties with social interaction on campus, problems in interaction with faculty or administration, lack of opportunities for part-time work or difficulties with housing or shopping as being the result of negative discriminatory attitudes of university staff, other students and people in the wider community.

They noted a distinction between the experiences of white English-speaking nationals (such as European, New Zealand or Canadian students) and the experiences of 'black' or non-white (such as Middle Eastern, Asian, Indian and Latin American) students. Whilst white international students rarely reported perceptions of discrimination in their social environment, non-white international students expressed perceptions of experiences of discomfort, verbal insults and also direct confrontation. Students reported degrees of disrespect towards them (depending on the context) within the university and outside in the community mainly based on cultural traits and language. One Mexican female student noted that she now understood that there are different degrees of racism and that some of them are predicated on negative attitudes to the way international students use the language, in this case English.

This research raises some further issues relating to the stereotyping of international students and attitudes to international students' approaches to learning. Through identifying what is seen as harmless stereotyping in such comments as 'they like to remain in their own groups' and 'they never contribute in class' as a form of neo-racism, Lee and Rice provoke thought. Their research makes a bold statement and could stimulate discussion of some uncomfortable issues, and this could be an important step towards changing perceptions of the role of international students in Higher Education.

It is interesting to note how the two research projects considered in this section show how research has moved on in this field. Bochner et al.'s (1977) article considers international students in an isolated context, that of the educational centre in which they studied. Their study does not interrogate the context in which international and home students interact. Lee and Rice (2007) see international students as part of a complex social context that extends beyond the university into the community. The later study considers the response of the host community to be responsible for social difficulties, as opposed to earlier views that may have attributed difficulties to individuals or groups of international students and their inability or unwillingness to adapt to their new context. Lee and Rice's holistic view of international students as part of the social fabric of the communities that surround the university is an important one and is resonant with the main research project that supports this book.

Large-scale research on international students: Examples from the UK and New Zealand

This section of the chapter considers two large-scale quantitative research projects which were carried out in the same year, 2004, in two different national contexts. Both of these projects chose a quantitative paradigm, one of the projects involving primary research and the other concentrating on secondary research, with literature review and document analysis forming an important part of the data. Both projects were initiated by government-funded organizations concerned, amongst other things, with the national brand of Higher Education in their particular context. The consideration of these two projects alongside each other presents a picture of the importance of social context in the experience of international students in two different national contexts. Both the methodologies and findings of these two projects provide an important setting for, and comparison with, the main research project of this book.

The social experiences of international students: UKCOSA study (2004)

A study involving 4,796 international students in UK Higher Education and Further Education was carried out by the Council for International Education (UKCOSA) in 2004. The study covers a large number of student responses in a wide range of institutions, with the vast majority of responses coming from Higher Education.

Respondents to the 2004 UKCOSA study consisted of international students on a range of course types and subjects (PG and UG) from 150 different (non-UK) countries, and they were given an extensive questionnaire that asked them to respond to issues relating to their experience and perceptions on their study and life in the UK.

For this book the most significant part of the study was that which interrogated students' views on their own 'social integration' and their perception of the UK. It found that international students were much more closely 'integrated' with students of their own nationality and with other international students, with 59% stating that most of their friendships were in that international category. Just 32% of the students in the study noted that their friends were a mixture of UK and international students, and a small minority of 7% said that they were friends with mainly UK students as opposed to international students.

It was also noted that 70% of taught postgraduate students stated that they had no UK friends, with the report suggesting that this could be attributable to the high proportion of international students in their classes. Fifty-one per cent of undergraduate students said that they had no UK friends, and students who were studying in subjects with a large concentration of international students were also less likely to have UK friends. The report supposed that this was consistent with the supposition that it is easier for international students to mix with the UK student group if the ratios are smaller (Merrick, 2004: 67).

Expectations about relationships

The report indicated that one of the most significant concerns for students before and after they arrived in the UK was worrying about being able to mix with home students. Approximately 41% of students said that they were worried about this issue and this was almost the highest percentage amongst the concerns, second only to accommodation. The data in the study showed that the students were more concerned about mixing with home students than they were about coping with course content. They were also less concerned about their relationships with academic staff (Merrick, 2004: 30). Indeed the UKCOSA data which was given by undergraduates showed that the concern over mixing with UK students was the most important worry for UG international students (Merrick, 2004: 32).

So it may be that expectations and preconceptions which international students have about the difficulty of interacting with home students could influence their interactions once they arrive at university. It was clear that one student in the UKCOSA study felt that these expectations had been proved right and she felt that there were significant barriers in both academic and social areas. The Indonesian female postgraduate noted:

> Tell us how to mix with UK people properly...because in fact there's lots of barriers to get close to them. Sometimes UK students underestimate international students' capabilities, and it's hard to work in a team with them because they always feel that they are in the right side in term of opinion and the way of thinking. (Merrick, 2004: 67)

The study also found that there were positive experiences once the negative expectations had been proven wrong. A Mexican male undergraduate in the study was quoted as saying the following:

> Well before I came I thought that all British people were very serious kind of dry very stiff culture, and that they were kind of racist, also I was worried that I would not make any friends (British) but since my arrival everything was different the people very polite, very patient because my English wasn't very good at the time, in university I met a lot of new friends, the staff were wonderful and it exceeded what I was expecting. (Merrick, 2004: 31)

The power of experience of intercultural interaction to change students' perceptions of working in an international context is a crucial element of the research presented in this book and has been demonstrated in previous studies (Volet and Ang, 1998).

The UKCOSA report noted that the relationship between staff and students was vital in influencing students' views of their experience at university. Some of the concerns that the international students in the survey had about interacting with UK students also appeared to be applied to their relationships with staff. Whilst there were many positive comments in the survey relating to staff–student relationships, there was also the sense that some of the preconceptions relating to relationships across cultures and nationalities had affected staff attitudes to students (and vice versa) (Teekens, 2006; Caglar, 2006). One Kenyan male postgraduate said:

> Lecturers/supervisors should not make assumptions about other people's cultures and use it against them. (Merrick, 2004: 28)

Who to talk to?

The UKCOSA survey asked who students would talk to about an academic problem and it is very significant to note that 67% of the students responded that they would talk to friends or fellow students about this academic difficulty. Indeed, also significantly, it was seen that students said that they would be equally likely to talk to family (35%) as to talk to their course leader (33%), despite the geographical distance. Where personal problems were concerned a large majority of students would discuss these with their friends or family (85%) and only 14% of students would have consulted a personal tutor with a personal problem. It is important to note this as it again underscores the significance of the international students' social network to their learning experience. It appears that friendship, kinship and academic issues are strongly bound together.

Language also appeared to be a major factor that influenced the perception of relationships of international students. The survey indicated a correlation between better language proficiency, 'integration' and levels of satisfaction with their experience. Students who had more advanced language competence were better integrated and also appeared to then be more satisfied with their time at university (Merrick, 2004: 48). The study also suggested a strong link between 'inter-group contact' between international students and UK students and a positive attitude to the experience as a whole.

Are international networks less useful?

Having raised some important issues from the UKCOSA report, it is significant to consider a particular section of the research that appears to suggest that networks of students that are solely international are in some way more limited than multinational networks. The 2004 study supports the suggestion that international students often have a group of co-nationals who provide them with personal support and that the friendship group of international students mostly consists of co-nationals and other international students. The UKCOSA study goes a step further and suggests that these international networks may in one way be less useful in terms of the quality of support they can give. The study says:

> This raises questions about the limitations which support networks will have if they consist mainly of co-nationals and other international students, whose familiarity with UK systems is likely to be lower than that of UK students. (Merrick, 2004: 68)

In contrast, the research that supports this book finds that the international student network is a useful and highly supportive set of ties, providing a strong academic and personal bond that adds to the quality of the international student's educational experience. Chapter 4 of this book shows how this international community of practice provides mutual social, academic and practical support.

Approaches to 'managing cultural diversity' in New Zealand (2004)

Ho, Holmes and Cooper produced a report for the Ministry of Education and Education New Zealand that reviewed literature and teaching practices around the issue of 'managing cultural diversity'. The review was an extensive one, with over 160 sources being considered, including books, government-commissioned reports, conference papers, journal articles and PhD theses from New Zealand and also from other countries worldwide.

The report was initiated in response to the increase in international students in a number of educational contexts including universities in New Zealand. It notes that students and staff in New Zealand were suddenly faced with cultural diversity in the classroom. Ho et al. state that it is interesting to note that it took a sudden increase in international students from overseas for there to be an acknowledgement of the multiculturalism represented by the indigenous Maori and Pasifika populations who were present in New Zealand long before international students began to travel the globe in larger numbers.

Working against the 'deficit approach'

The report highlights cultural influences on educational traditions and on teaching, learning and educational practices. It stresses the need to counteract the deficit approach to international students and the importance of valuing and celebrating cultural difference in education. It presents one of its goals as being to develop 'culturally responsive' classrooms that question and challenge the assumptions and attitudes of both teachers and students towards culture and knowledge. Furthermore, these classrooms would need to begin

> accommodating multiple perspectives and voices; questioning prior assumptions about teaching and learning; creating an inclusive learning environment; and examining the behaviours of teachers and teacher language. (2004: xiii)

The report aims to enable teachers and students to engage in reflection on their own culture and on the cultures of others in order to create opportunities for socialization between all groups in education. The role of language and communication is seen as an area that requires 'nurturing and monitoring' by both teachers and students in order to achieve intercultural socialization. Ho et al. emphasize that the educational philosophies reviewed in the literature can be of benefit to all students, not just international students but all students involved in education in New Zealand.

Collectivist vs individualist cultures?

There is one aspect of the report that is interesting to discuss. Ho et al. refer to the concept of collectivist versus individualist societies in their approach to diversity in education. As discussed in detail in Chapter 1, the principle of the collectivist or the individualist society is an idea that suggests that whole national societies can be said to behave in uniform and patterned ways (Hofstede, 1984). It suggests that values said to be inherent in particular cultures (such as promoting the needs of the collective group over the individual) can powerfully influence the behaviour of individuals. Collectivist cultures are defined as being East and South Asians, Africans, Latin Americans, and South Europeans, whereas individualist cultures are said to be New Zealanders, Australians, North and West Europeans, and North Americans from European backgrounds (Ho et al., 2004: ix). The world is thus divided into two parts and it is suggested that individual human behaviour can be categorized along these binaries. Furthermore, there is a suggestion that shared cultural values from these enormously wide geographical groupings could be a driving influence in students' approaches to learning. Ho et al. note that:

> In collectivist cultures, students accept that they must cooperate and support the teacher at all times. They tend to avoid confrontation in class. In individualist societies where face consciousness

> is weak, giving correct information is more important than saving one's face. (2004: ix)

These statements that make links between these geographical groupings and behaviour in the classroom appear to disregard the factors of family backgrounds, age, ethnic diversity within countries or cultures, individual preferences and the influence of different learning environments. It is likely that students from the same geographical region, the same nationality and the same city might respond differently in a classroom as a result of variation in other crucial factors that make up their personal learning 'culture'.

Dialectic vs dialogic 'cultures' of teaching?

Ho et al. also raise the issue of approaches to teaching and delivery in the classroom, particularly the dialectic versus the dialogic way of teaching. They note that dialectic approaches to teaching are teacher-centred and focus on the transmission of knowledge, whereas dialogic approaches are more student-centred, emphasizing interaction and the social construction of knowledge. Ho et al. imply that collectivist societies or 'non-western' societies favour a dialectic approach to teaching where *'students are very rarely allowed to interact with one another or with the teacher in the classroom'* (2004: 7). Further to this, Confucian Heritage Cultures (CHC) are defined as groups of South East Asian countries that are assumed to be unquestioning adherents to dialectic teaching. Ho et al. note:

> Current Chinese educational systems still retain a dialectic mode which encourages competition between students and the complete authority of the teacher. (ibid.)

These assumptions about the teaching and learning contexts of whole countries might encourage a categorization of groups of learners. It could certainly be said that there exist educational contexts or even individual teachers in the UK that still retain an emphasis on the 'dialectic mode'. However, approaches to teaching are as patterned and varied as approaches to learning, and teachers might employ dialectic or dialogic teaching to suit a particular learning context or a certain body of knowledge or part of their course. It is unlikely that one teacher in the UK or in China would teach entirely in one mode or the other.

The New Zealand report classifies the Maori and Pasifika cultures as collectivist cultures and relates some aspects of their response to learning (for example a duality between home and school) back to tribal origins and events prior to the arrival of missionaries in New Zealand (2004: 8). Whilst the report acknowledges the complexity of the Maori and Pasifika social and cultural context, it does not acknowledge that within these groups there could be varied and complex responses to their learning in Higher Education.

Ho et al. acknowledge that all students of all backgrounds may utilize deep, surface or strategic learning approaches. Research has shown that learners can employ deep approaches in one context and surface or strategic approaches in another, depending on how students are encouraged to behave by institutional and teaching and learning approaches to areas such as assessment (Gannon-Leary and Smailes, 2004). However, the report also notes that international students who may come from CHC backgrounds or collectivist cultures may have difficulty in 'adapting' to the 'interactive' and 'game-loving' style of 'western teaching' in New Zealand. The use of these categories could encourage preconceptions about groups of learners, leading away from a focus on the complexity of social and cultural backgrounds.

Whilst values and social backgrounds evidently will exert an influence on approaches to education, more emphasis should be placed on variation of responses within ethnic and national groups of students. Much more in the vein of the research carried out by Lee and Rice (2007), approaches to diversity must be about sharing responsibility for promoting intercultural communication with all parties involved, including institutions and societies, and not attributing difficulties to generalities about group or national cultures. The discussion of Ho et al.'s report is intended to underline the importance of understanding the complexity of the learning environment as a setting that may influence and change students' approaches to learning from classroom to classroom across one institution and in response to the individualism of the teacher.

International students and approaches to learning

There is a range of research that focuses on international students' approaches to learning (Biggs, 1999; Cortazzi and Jin, 2006; De Vita, 2001). A great deal of the research is problem-oriented and concentrates on international students' perceived difficulties with adapting to Higher Education in a foreign country. Leonard et al. (2004) note that when looking at some aspects of the research into international students it is striking to note the amount of research that concentrates on 'the problems' of international students and their 'need for help'.

In particular, some of the research concentrates on international students' 'adaptation' in terms of their approaches to learning, and there is an implication that students simply apply their previous approaches to their new context without thought to the relevance or applicability of these approaches. Spurling (2006) notes that the main weakness of the literature in this field is that it indicates that adjustment is essential but does not define what this might mean within the specific Higher Education academic context. This section considers some of the research that relates to international students' approaches to learning.

Deep and surface learning and international students

A well-established view of the idea of learning relates to the ideas of 'surface' and 'deep' approaches. In the 1970s Ference Marton investigated a common academic task, reading academic articles, using a naturalistic approach. The research looked at the defining features of approaches to learning that emerged from this reading and from qualitative interviews with students (Marton, Hounsell and Entwistle, 1997: 19). Three definitions of approaches to learning emerged from this research: a deep approach which was considered 'transformative'; a surface approach which was viewed as 'reproductive'; and a strategic approach which was thought to be associated with 'organized' approaches to achieving the highest grades (ibid.). The overall implication from the research indicated that the deep approaches produced a more lasting and meaningful outcome than surface approaches (ibid.).

Later research by Marton and Saljo acknowledges that the relationship between the process and outcome of learning is a complex one. Manipulating learning environments in order to produce deep approaches to learning may not necessarily produce the outcomes that are intended. Learning is a complex interaction of wide-ranging factors, many of which are established before the student enters the learning environment, and the suggestion that there is a deterministic context that can easily be changed to produce the right learning outcomes is an over-simplified view. Indeed, two students in the same teaching and learning environment may well adopt opposite approaches to their learning (Haggis, 2003).

A parallel perception of the idea of surface and deep learning approaches is suggested by Mann (2001). She suggests a view of learning that shifts the emphasis from deep or surface approach to 'engagement and alienation', terms that encompass the sociocultural context of the learning process. Mann concentrates on the issue of alienation, a form of 'estrangement' from involvement in the content and process of study, and intimates that one of the causes of this alienation is the contemporary ethos of commercialism, efficiency and utilitarianism in Higher Education. This emphasis on measurement and 'performativity' leads to an instrumental view of the education process, and this in itself alienates the learner from the more meaningful and complex aspects of their learning (Mann, 2001: 8–9).

Mann suggests that all students are 'outsiders' as they come into HE, as they are not immersed in the discourse of the context. Interestingly, she notes that it is as if students were crossing into another country. She says:

> Most students entering the new world of the academy are in an equivalent position to those crossing the borders of a new country – they have to deal with the bureaucracy of checkpoints, or matriculation, they may have limited knowledge of the local language and customs, and are alone. (2001: 11)

This is an interesting view, as it suggests that alienation from learning is linked to a social and psychological estrangement that is similar to geographic and cultural transition, an experience familiar to the international student.

The issue of approaches to learning in the case of international students appears to be confused by the fact that there is an implied link between approaches to learning and culture. For example, Ho et al.'s report, discussed above, suggests that approaches to learning such as deep, surface and strategic are associated with certain cultures, and indeed a further step is often taken to make a link between approaches to learning, culture and then nationality. For example, references to CHC complicate and confuse the issue of international students' approaches to learning by associating Chinese students' approaches to learning with one single set of philosophies of Chinese history. There are many other philosophers and influences on Chinese learning, such as Taoism. The suggestion that Chinese students' approaches to learning in a Higher Education context abroad are entirely governed by Confucian Heritage Cultures is similar to the suggestion that British students respond to educational environments in the way that they do because of their Celtic heritage, because of Shakespeare or because of the influence of learning traditions from the Enlightenment era.

Memorization, critical thinking and international students

The role of memorization is seen to be linked to the transfer of CHC and seems to be a prominent feature of some views of the approaches to learning of all international students, not just Chinese or South East Asian students. CHC may play a part in some students' approaches to learning, but this does not mean that students will uniformly approach their learning in Higher Education according to this influence alone. Memorization was for a long time considered a valid learning practice in 'western' educational contexts (Vandermensbrugghe, 2004). From a personal point of view as someone who left British education 25 years ago my primary and early secondary school education consisted of a great deal of memorization: of maths tables, of poetry and of Latin verb conjugations. This aspect of my previous learning experience does not appear to have precluded me from approaching learning according to the particular context, responding with analysis or critical approaches as the situation has dictated.

The idea of memorization or rote learning is often viewed as a 'surface' approach. However, in studies involving Chinese students who were high educational achievers, memorization appeared to be used in a manner that led to understanding, and this is seen as the 'deep' approach. This was termed the 'Chinese Paradox' (Marton and Trigwell, 2000). Tang (1994: 10) also draws attention to the possible link between memorization and comprehension and she terms this 'deep memorization', a combination of understanding and rote learning. These ideas suggest that theories of deep and surface learning should not be seen as binary concepts but should be considered to be linked in a complex relationship.

The discussion above underlining the complexity of how students respond in the Higher Educational learning environment points to the invalidity of the links between rote learning, surface approaches and particular international student groups. Responses in the educational environment are highly complex, and studies which have attempted to apply models of approaches to learning in other cultural contexts have found that some of their fundamental concepts have been contradicted (Haggis, 2003).

International students, criticality and plagiarism

Spurling (2006) reports that there is considerable vagueness in concepts relating to the learning of international students. For example, it is often assumed that international students are not able to engage with critical thinking tasks because of the influence of their educational background. Recent research carried out by Vandermensbrugghe (2004) notes that ideas of criticality are not understood uniformly by staff, let alone by students, international or otherwise. He states:

> The idea that the ability to think critically is required to do well at university is widespread, but the concept is vague and does not seem to have the same meaning for everybody, in every circumstance. (2004: 419)

Despite the fact that 'criticality' is highly prized in Higher Education, it is not clear that we all agree on what this might mean. Turner also notes that definitions of critical thinking are frequently unclear and stem from cultural knowledge traditions, not from 'universal measures of higher learning' (Turner, 2006: 3). In her study of a small group of Chinese students' experience of teaching and learning, Turner notes that the students were negatively characterized as having limited learning potential because of their 'inability to be critical'. In fact, when this was interrogated, it became apparent that students' underachievement could be attributed to the implicit nature of assessment criteria. Ideas of the nature of criticality may also vary across disciplines and across educational contexts. The assumption that criticality does not happen in universities outside 'western' education systems is not based on any evidence.

Alongside issues of how international students deal with criticality is the idea of their susceptibility to engagement with plagiarism. There seems to be a perception that international students' previous teaching and learning backgrounds or their approaches to learning render them much more likely to plagiarize in their writing or research. Plagiarism or 'cheating' (like 'criticality') should be recognized as a 'culturally determined concept' (McLean and Ransom, 2005). The 'rules' that are broken when someone 'cheats' are context-dependent and not always made explicit, and in Higher Education the 'rules' of writing and assessment are not automatically understood by students, international or otherwise. These are context-specific academic practices that need to be learned.

There is a wide range of literature that considers international students' difficulties with plagiarism (Leask, 2004). This appears to be reinforced by recent educational press coverage of the issue of plagiarism and 'cheating', spreading an almost endemic panic about the issue of plagiarism across the Higher Educational sector. There appears to be no evidence to indicate that it is more common for international students to plagiarize than home students. Research carried out by Barrett and Malcolm (2006) indicated exactly the opposite, and showed that students from undergraduate study in China were far less likely to plagiarize than students who did their undergraduate study in the UK. This result indicates that common associations between international students and plagiarism are not necessarily based on evidence, and Barrett and Malcolm's work completely contradicts popular 'cultural expectations of plagiarism' (Caruana, 2006: 63).

Thus, the response to the issues of plagiarism and critical thinking underlines the fact that these educational values are contextual and need to be taught and embedded in teaching, learning and assessment systems. Associating lack of critical thinking skills or understandings of plagiarism with international students' approaches to learning simply shifts the blame for these responses to unfamiliar educational contexts and to the individual student rather than considering how issues such as criticality and plagiarism can be designed into or out of institutional approaches to teaching, learning and assessment.

Language, identity and their influence on the context of learning

This section will consider some research that relates to language and identity and examine the relevance of this to the international student experience.

There is a very strong correlation between language, culture and identity. What we say, how we say it and who we are appear to be issues that are very difficult to isolate from each other. Language could be said to be at the centre and the basis of our interaction with others, and of course this is a crucial factor in the experience of international students. Bakhtin and Lacan have, with reference to Freud, suggested that language formulates our identity but also that without a symbolic identity we cannot develop language (Lechte, 1994: 68). Language is a medium through which others understand us and thus it is inextricably linked with who we are perceived to be.

Language is a means of expressing and also constructing one's identity and so is a highly significant element in our interactions and our relationships with others. Use of language is likely to influence the way we are perceived by others (Sysoyev, 2002). It might be said that a lack of language proficiency would make our identities difficult both to assert and to be perceived. Language is a form of social and cultural capital, and this form of capital may be a resource that allows access to understanding and being understood. A lack of language proficiency could also be associated with a lack of understanding and thus potentially mistaken for an inability to understand. In the case of international students it may be that lower language proficiency could be viewed by some as a lack of knowledge of subject or as lower academic potential (Trahar, 2007).

Another question that is raised by this discussion of language is whether there is a difference between the processes at work in language learning and in learning of subject knowledge. Is there a difference in the sort of learning that is going on when students are acquiring language and when they are learning the content of a particular academic discipline? It should be noted here that for the international student the learning of language and the learning of subject knowledge may be indivisible and could be viewed as part of the social learning experience. This multiple learning that is occurring for international students in their new environment is an integral part of the participation in a whole learning experience. Byram and Fleming (1998) suggest that learning a language means learning about its culture. They state:

> We would argue that linguistic and cultural learning are integrated. (1998: 44)

Perhaps even more significantly, learning the content of a specific academic discipline also involves learning about the cultural assumptions implicit in that content.

Chomsky's (1965) theory of an ideal native speaker was followed by Dell Hymes' (1972) notion of communicative competence, 'paying special attention to the sociolinguistic component, which connected language and culture' (Sysoyev, 2002). The concept of 'communicative competence' was further developed by Byram (1998) to include 'intercultural competence' and this idea strongly emphasized the significance of developing cultural knowledge as a means of both developing language competence and enabling the speaker to develop cross-cultural understanding.

The notion of the native speaker as the ideal to which every language learner should aspire has been criticized in recent years as English has spread across the globe and it is no longer the case that native speakers are born into a monocultural and monolinguistic context that gives them a birthright to the title of native speaker (Kramsch, 1998). As people move across borders with more frequency, their first language is no longer the property of the nation state. For example, the many varieties of English are now seen to be owned by their respective speakers and they need no longer aspire to a standard English set by the native speaker. Kramsch notes:

> In our days of frequent border crossings, and of multilingual multicultural foreign language classrooms, it is appropriate to rethink the monolingual native speaker norm ... I propose that we make the intercultural speaker the unmarked form, the infinite of language use, and the monolingual monocultural speaker a slowly disappearing species or a nationalistic myth. (1998: 30)

To apply the above idea to the ideas of this book, it may be suggested that intercultural learning (or learning about the 'other' both within ourselves and in others (Kristeva, 1991)) should become the norm of the internationalized university. In the same way as the native speaker should no longer be the norm, perhaps international students should no longer solely aspire to learn about British culture or from the British student as the ideal. Instead intercultural learning should become the goal for all students.

A further question that should be asked in relation to the topic of language is whether language learning has an automatic corollary of learning about culture. As it is difficult to separate the boundaries between language and culture (and again context plays a large part in this), it is equally difficult to divide the processes which are developing when a person learns a language and also learns about the culture or local practices which are part of that language context. If it is true, then, that when a person learns about language they also learn about culture, it may be that people proficient in more than one language (i.e. another language in addition to their mother tongue or tongues) are more aware of the differences and diversity that exist amongst people. Thus it may be that being exposed to language learning makes a person more tolerant of other people and their differences (Edwards, 1995). In this way it may be the case that international students arriving in another country have already developed a cultural awareness through their language learning. This may distinguish them in outlook from home students who may not have learned another language to any level of proficiency and who may not have had contact with people from other diverse communities.

A related question thus arises from this issue: does learning another language strengthen or diminish students' sense of national identity? It is clear that education can alter a person's perception of him or herself, and in this way it can be said that education may change our sense of who we are in relation to others. This paints a picture of a changing and developing social learning environment that is constructed as we construct ourselves and others. Nippert-Eng states that 'classificatory boundaries are the most essential element of culture' (1995: xi). This suggests that differences in culture are a matter of conceptual borders marked out and changed by the people who create them. As social contexts change so do the individual and societal perceptions of cultural and national boundaries. For example, a student noting his or her nationality as Soviet in 1988 may now class him or herself as Uzbek, Turkmen or Kazakh. It may be that learning about language and culture is a stronger force even than other forms of education for changing our view of ourselves and those with whom we live and work.

An interesting angle on the issue of identity and interaction across national borders is that presented by the work of Kristeva (1991). This work draws on the French existentialist movement, with echoes in the writings of Sartre and particularly of Albert Camus' *L'Etranger* (*The Stranger*). Kristeva maintains that the mistrust, fear and prejudice that surround our interactions with other cultures or groups are built out of a fear of 'the other' in ourselves. When we are in contact with a 'foreigner', our consciousness of hidden aspects of our own identity is raised, and it is our hatred of the strange within us that initiates conflict toward others. Kristeva notes:

> Strangely, the foreigner lives within us: he is the hidden face of our identity, the space that wrecks our abode, the time in which understanding and affinity founder ... The foreigner comes in when the consciousness of my difference arises, and he disappears when we all acknowledge ourselves as foreigners, unamenable to bonds and community. (1991: 1)

The existential argument is that the human condition precludes a true affinity or link with others. Kristeva notes that it is this realization that comes to the surface when we are faced by the difference in others. Kristeva also interestingly questions the possibilities in a new world order that means we are in contact with other nationalities. She suggests that if we are to interact successfully with others on a global scale we have to learn to reconcile our own identity and difference.

So Kristeva suggests that our views of others must change if we are to derive the most benefit from the new global community. Indeed, to achieve the idea of a global tolerance, it will be necessary to recognize this 'otherness' in our selves and in others, and indeed, as Byram and Fleming note, to reach a state in which we can 'identify with otherness' (1998: 5). Once we have developed this skill to see, understand and accept difference in ourselves and others and 'see the common humanity beneath it', we become an 'intercultural speaker' (Byram and Fleming, 1998: 8). Intercultural speakers have knowledge of more than language and the way it works; they have developed a competence in interacting with people who are different from and the same as themselves, and it may be that this development may fit them for a future living and working in a wider global community.

Summary

The discussions of this chapter have underlined the fact that friendships and social relationships are a significant element of the learning experience. The research examined here has also indicated that the context in which learning takes place can exert an influence on relationships that develop at university and in the community that surrounds Higher Education (Bochner et al., 1977; Lee and Rice, 2007). Furthermore, where students still hold negative preconceptions about each other (Merrick, 2004) and assumptions are made about previous learning experiences (Ho et al., 2004) opportunities are being missed for the building of a collaborative international learning culture.

Learning about others is presented here as a crucial element of the experience of Higher Education in an internationalized world. Language was discussed here as being a highly significant part of this. However, further discussion in Chapters 5 and 8 of this book will emphasize the fact that it is not simply language proficiency that is the key to intercultural interaction. Rather, a more complex picture of what it means to be an intercultural person, including previous experiences of other cultures and the ability to communicate with 'the other', is considered.

This issue will be taken up again in Chapter 8 of this book when recent research is examined that suggests that in innovative, collaborative teaching and learning environments intercultural learning is being viewed as a positive and integral element of the learning experience (Montgomery, 2009).

Part 2
The Research

3 Student Voices, Student Lives: International Students in Context

The aim of this chapter is to present some 'real' profiles of international students, built on data gathered in the research that supports this book. There are seven portraits of international students from a range of nationalities: Chinese, Indonesian, Nepalese, Dutch, Italian and Indian. The students differ in age, in social and educational background and in academic disciplines. The links between these students are not related to nationality but to their friendship, as they are part of a linked social network. Presenting a friendship group foregrounds characteristics of the students' social experience and takes the focus of attention away from nationality groupings. This will contextualize the students' experience and provide richer conceptions of students that will combat some of the stereotypes that are associated with international students and their experience in Higher Education. As Hollway and Jefferson point out 'When we aggregate people, treating diversity as error variable, in search of what is common to all, we often learn about what is true of no one in particular' (2000:8).

The profiles included here are drawn from the extensive observations and shadowing activity that are part of this research. Such ethnographically inflected data is not easy to present in readable form: the challenge is to distil more than 200 hours spent over six months as part of the student group into organized, digestible sections. The researcher followed the students in their everyday life at university, going with them to lectures, tutorials, to the library, to lunch and to the pub. The process of recording, analysing and explaining the chaotic experience of everyday life is a problematic one and inevitably involves stages of interpretation that distance the researcher and then the reader from the events. However difficult it is to explain such experience in a satisfactory way, it will be attempted here, as familiarity with the 'characters' who will speak in the following chapters of the book is important to the reader's contextualized understanding of what the students say. In addition, this chapter is representative of the distinctive approach of this study, which aims to promote a strongly contextualized and empirical understanding of student experience. The section below on the importance of the methodology will provide more detail on the thinking behind the approach.

The vignettes of experience are written in a narrative and reflective style that mirrors the informal manner in which the data was collected. A narrative inquiry approach to studying and understanding diversity can be one of the most involving forms of learning about it, and has the potential to foster 'sensitive learning and teaching in a multicultural higher education landscape' (Trahar, 2007: 24). The profiles presented in this chapter are intended to develop this sort of understanding of diversity.

The chapter presents seven profiles that describe the participants, and these are not entirely uniform in their explanations, just as the people are not uniform. The profiles are followed by four descriptions of experiences in particular contexts: in a bar, in two classrooms and in the Chess Club, a Student Union society. These are four examples amongst many experiences in different contexts, and are not intended to be representative but to give a flavour of the student experience recorded in the extended shadowing project.

Figure 1 below shows a network diagram that introduces the students and indicates with arrows the relationships between them.

The importance of the methodology

As the discussion of research in the previous chapter has shown, there are examples of large-scale research projects about the international student experience, but projects that examine a particular aspect using qualitative, ethnographic methods are rare. The choice of methodology in research can indicate a particular way of thinking about an issue: the approaches of the UKCOSA study (Merrick, 2004) and the 'Managing Cultural Diversity Study' from New Zealand (Ho et al., 2004) achieved the presentation of a broad picture of a large number of international students in a wide range of different contexts. This approach indicates an emphasis on the student group as a whole. In contrast, the research supporting this book concentrates on only a small number of students in one particular context and examines their experience in great detail. This suggests an emphasis on the significance of the individual student

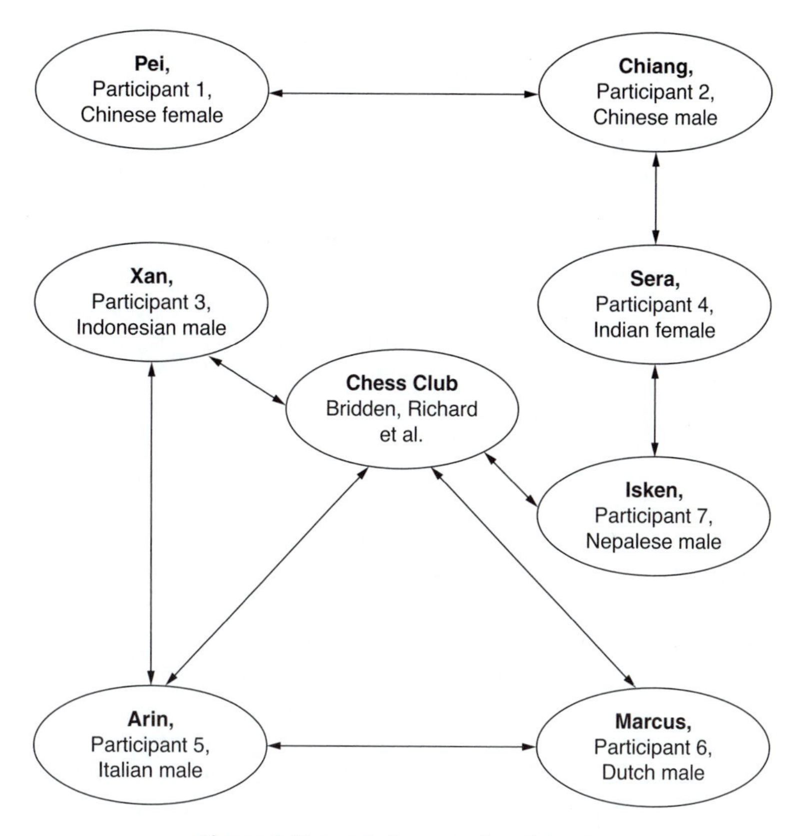

Figure 1 Network diagram of participants

in context. Both approaches are, of course, valid, and both are required if we are to gain a credible understanding of the experience of international students.

The research supporting this book takes what is commonly understood as a 'constructivist approach', which assumes that the constructed views of the student are what make up the 'truth' of his or her situation. This approach acknowledges that both researchers and researched are involved in co-construction of knowledge (Strauss and Corbin, 1994). Altheide and Johnson (1994) note that ethnographic research aims to 'see first-hand what occurs' and through this provide 'knowledge as understanding' (1994: 487). This research seeks an 'interpretive validity' where the ethic is to aim for a critical commitment to present participants' understandings and contexts. After all, the social world is an interpreted world rather than a literal one, and because of this it is always undergoing a symbolic construction (Altheide and Johnson, 1994: 489).

The limitations of the approach

As with all research methodologies, there are limitations and drawbacks to each approach. In the case of qualitative ethnographically inflected approaches such as those taken in this study, the focus is on a small number of participants in a particular context. As a result, there are challenges associated with the potential for generalizability of the specific findings of a small group of individuals in one particular context. This sort of research does not claim that the small sample chosen is representative of all international students, but that in similar contexts with similar groups of students there may be parallels. In order that such comparison is possible, a section below provides some detailed information about the context in which this research took place.

A further criticism of the sort of approaches taken in this research is related to the subjectivity inherent in the role of the researcher. Alvesson and Skoldberg (2000: 1) note the fact that 'knowledge cannot be separated from the knower', and thus we must acknowledge the role of subjectivity and personal interpretation in research. As advances have been made in qualitative and ethnographic research there has been a move away from seeing researcher involvement as a problem towards acknowledging researcher-as-participant as an active and crucial element in this sort of research. Because ethnography tries to portray the complexity of the world around us and the multiplex relationship between people, it is essential that the researcher is seen as part of that complexity. Thus in such interpretivist research it is important that the researcher and their own background and cultural perspective are acknowledged, as this will influence the research and its presentation. To this end, Appendix 2 of this book provides a profile of the researcher that details her background and accounts for how and why this research was initiated.

The shadowing project

The information presented in this chapter draws upon the shadowing data of the research. Shadowing, following a given participant in his or her everyday life, is an observation method that is used in a range of Social Science research, not simply as a triangulation technique but as a means of gaining 'a richer, pluralistic view of the research setting' (McDonald, 2005: 461), since it allows the researcher access to observe settings and situations that she would otherwise not have permission to enter. Shadowing also enables the researcher to see the context being studied at first hand and experience it contemporaneously in much the same way that the participant is experiencing it. The researcher is able to view the context of the participant but also to experience his or her opinions and behaviour simultaneously through the commentary provided by the participant within the context (McDonald, 2005: 457).

There are, of course, some difficulties associated with the method of shadowing, including negotiating access with participants. In the case of this study this entailed negotiating access to lectures and tutorials through the students' lecturers and tutors. Factors which affect other observation methods also apply to the method of shadowing, most notably the observer's paradox or the 'Hawthorne effect', which relates to how the presence of the researcher affects the behaviour of the participants within the context (Shipman, 1997, cited in McDonald, 2005: 459). However, extended periods of shadowing can combat this to some extent by what Lincoln and Guba (1985) term 'persistent observation', where familiarity with the presence of the researcher makes him or her progressively less intrusive. As discussed above, one of the most difficult aspects of the use of shadowing in research is the amount of data it can produce and the way in which this data is handled and presented.

The context for the study: A brief demographic background

In order for the reader to be able to compare his or her own institutional context with the one being discussed here, some demographic background to the university where the research took place is important. The university is a UK institution which gained university status in 1992 (what is known in the UK as a 'new university'). In keeping with similar HE institutions, it has dramatically increased its numbers of international students in the last 15 years. At the time of the study international students accounted for approximately 13% of the total number of students and there were plans for this to increase. It is interesting to note the spread of nationalities across the university and the development of specific 'markets' for international recruitment. The information in the table below is taken from a survey, *The International Student Barometer (ISB)*, carried out on behalf of a consortium of universities (2005). The table shows the numbers of students in the six

Table 1 Spread of the six main nationalities

Total number of international students	*3753*
China	959
Malaysia	387
India	212
Germany	133
France	81
Nigeria	75

biggest nationality groups in the academic year in which the research took place and the total number of international students present in the university. It is worth noting that there are a total of 95 different nationalities in the university but the students are clustered in the nationalities shown in Table 1. Many of the 95 nations have numbers of students below 10.

The data collected by the ISB also indicates that there is not a great imbalance in gender, with 54% of students being male and 46% being female. In terms of choice of subject area, the ISB survey shows a clustering of international students in the areas of Business Studies, Engineering, Mathematics and Computing Sciences and an increased interest in Law.

The ISB study pointed out that the university in which the research took place resembles similar UK 'new universities' in terms of its numbers of international students and its range of nationalities. It is useful to note that countries such as China and India are growing international markets for universities attempting to attract international students in larger numbers.

Choice of network

In the choice of participants for the study it was considered important to select students who had spent around one year in the UK and had thus passed the initial stages of settling in and developing a social group. In addition to this, it was considered important that the students were selected not according to their nationality but according to their friendship network and variables such as age and course. As discussed in Chapter 2, the issues of nationality and culture can be misleading, and thus it was decided to choose these students across nationality, relying on a social network rather than any politically constructed divisions of nationality.

Thus, a social network of students who had been in the UK for around a year or two years was targeted and a network with a mix of undergraduates and postgraduates chosen. In the selected friendship group the students who were undergraduates were mainly in their second or third year of study. The age range was between 23 and 28 years, and the variation was a result of differences in educational systems in particular countries which meant that students varied in age across nationality groups. There was only one student, Arin, who was more mature, at the age of 28. A conscious decision was made not to select a network of research students on PhD courses, as these students were considered to be likely to be mature students living with families and would thus constitute quite a different social group.

The student profiles

Pei

> I think I am an outgoing person. I'd like to get to know more people. I think I am independent and I normally get to know others very quickly but I can manage most of my own things. If I didn't know these friends I think I could get to know others.

Pei is a 24-year-old Chinese female, an only child, from Zheng Zhou, the capital city of Henan Province in the middle region of China. She is in her second year at university, having done a BA final year and presently studying a Postgraduate International Business course. Pei lived in a university residence where many international students chose to live, as it consisted of self-contained flats at a reasonable price. The building was situated in an economically deprived area and inhabited by around 95% international students of a wide range of nationalities. Whilst Pei lived in the city she studied at a small satellite campus of the university, 18 miles north of the city in a remote rural area. She travelled to this campus by university bus on the days on which she had classes.

Pei's friends

Pei had a small group of close friends, the main core of this group being four Chinese female students. She knew three of these female students when she was in China as they were friends at college there and came to university together. Two of these female students were doing the same course as Pei and another of the female students shared a flat with Pei. These five female students spent most of the time together as they all lived in the same residence and travelled to university together by bus.

Pei had become involved in a Christian group through a local Parish Church and an International Student Café (the Glade), a meeting place set up by the church specifically for international students. Through this Christian group she made what she considered to be a close friend, Joan, an English woman who invited her to the group. Joan had four other English friends whom Pei knew and who were all members of the Christian group. Pei had also met some other students through participating in a Bible study group; three of these were also Chinese students at the university. Pei was not a Christian and had no intention of becoming one but said she attended the group because it helped her to improve her English and make more friends.

She also had another group of friends, six or seven in number, whom she met while working part time on the university's meet and greet programme (meeting other international students on their arrival at the airport). Pei also included in her list of friends and contacts her mother and father and cousins, who were back in China, and her boyfriend, who lived in America. She was in frequent contact with these geographically distant networks via email.

Reflection

Although Pei had a small group of close friends she also demonstrated a level of social independence. She sat with close friends in classes but between classes she tended to move around the campus alone and followed her own agenda of things she had to do. Pei's days seemed to be dominated by going to lectures, then going to the library or more often computer rooms. Pei seemed to use cafes and food outlets less frequently than other students. She brought her own drinks and said she often waited until she got home to cook Chinese food with friends. I assumed that this was an issue of cost, but not going to the cafes provided fewer opportunities for mixing on social lines with other students, home or international.

Pei recalled during an interview that there was a trip to Edinburgh that she wanted to go on but her close group of friends did not want to go. She said she did want to go and her friends asked her 'If we don't go will you still go?' When she said yes her friends were unhappy with her. She still went on the trip and met some new people and some people she hadn't seen for a long time. She was glad she had gone. When I asked her if she relied on her close group of friends to support her in order that she could be successful in her course, she disagreed. She said she felt that she could do it alone and if she didn't have that group of friends she could make some others.

Pei's friendship group consisted mainly of female friends. The male contacts in her group were mainly boyfriends of her female friends. She tended to sit with all-female groups during classes. In contrast to this, the academic staff of her department were mainly male and mainly regional or local in their background.

Xan

> I like to make friends with everybody – that's part of my personality. I know a lot of people from different backgrounds. When I first came to England the way I thought was different but now if someone says something I think of the reason behind it – what do they mean and I more easily respect them and the differences in people.

Xan is an Indonesian male aged 24 from Surabaya, in his second year at university, studying in the final year of a Master's in Business and Information Technology. He has one younger sister, who is still at home in Indonesia. Xan lived at a local campus three miles from the city site of the university where there were a number of university-owned halls of residence. Xan was finishing his Master's dissertation and he was no longer attending lectures when we met.

Xan's friends

Xan appeared to know a large number of people. As he walked through campus he often spoke to other students and a wide range of students recognized him. Xan said that he had many friends and these fell into different groups. He had a group of Indonesian friends who formed the Indonesian society of students from two local universities. He had a girlfriend whom he met through this society, and she was also Indonesian and studied at the same university as Xan. He said he also had a group of local home student friends and this included his Scottish friend, with whom he often went fishing. Xan had an extensive, mainly male-oriented friendship group that appeared to consist of many nationalities. He also had a base of friends of his own nationality in the Indonesian society of two local universities. He was a member of the Chess Club, a Student Union society.

Reflection

Xan appeared confident and sociable, and, judging from how many students he greeted around campus, he seemed to have a wide range of contacts and was popular with other students. He appeared to feel confident with his surroundings and comfortable in his conversation both with friends and with his tutor. At the same time he appeared to be independent and, like Pei, moved around campus individually rather than attached to another friend or group of contacts. His interest in chess and his confidence academically suggested that he was intellectually motivated and thoughtful, although he also had an interest in sport and played football with a mixed group of UK and international students on his residential campus. Despite this contact with male home students through the football games, these relationships had not developed into close friendships. Xan considered this to be related to the time he had known these male students but also to the language barrier.

Xan had experience of living and working in London when he first came to the UK. He made some friends and seemed to learn a lot about being in a new cultural environment when he was there. He laughed about the things he did when he was in London and seemed to see a difference in himself now compared with then in terms of his experience and knowledge of living abroad in a new culture.

Xan had some well-considered ideas about his home culture and the dichotomies between 'East and West' and modern and traditional cultures, especially as they related to religion and Islam. He talked about the great cultural difference within his own nationality. He compared the older generations with younger, the traditional with modern and extremely religious people with moderates. His example of the contemporary 'belly-dancer' who was then popular with some in Indonesia was an interesting one. She had caused a national controversy and extensive discussion between the different social groups in Indonesia as to whether her dancing was art or pornography. Xan also said that some of the Indonesian students who come to the UK were extremely religious and he felt he could not relate to them when they were here in the UK any more than he could when they were all back home in Indonesia.

Xan appeared to have developed these ideas and a striking awareness about how people are the same and different across nationalities through his experiences of living abroad, having the opportunity to reflect on the comparative differences between the countries he had lived in.

Chiang

> I prefer to make friends with students from different countries because I can [get to know] their culture [and] practise my English. But if it's a Chinese friend I make I prefer to make friends from the same city as me like Shanghai, actually ... I don't want to make friends with people from other parts of China.

Chiang is a 24-year-old Chinese male from Shanghai. He is in year 3 of an undergraduate Business Administration course and in his second year at university, having come directly into year 2 of his course. Chiang lived on the university's city campus in a self-catering hall of residence. Like Pei, he studies at one of the satellite campuses of the university and travels there by bus (18 miles) on the days when he has classes.

Chiang's friends

Chiang had a large number of people whom he knew in the UK, but he said that he did not have a close set of friends. He said that his own preference was to get to know a lot of people but he did not get very close to anyone in particular. Chiang was recognized by a lot of students as he walked around campus. He had a group of Chinese friends who were on his course, and he had some passing relationships and contact with some of the home students too. He chatted to them and saw them at the university gym.

Chiang explained that he had a conscious approach to choosing whom he liked to make friends with, and he said that the reasons behind this were to do with his background. He preferred not to make friends with Chinese students who were not from Shanghai, and he said his parents would not like it if he did because this would not improve his English and this is why they had sent him to England. He also expressed a preference for international rather than home students as friends in the academic environment, and talked about language as a barrier to really getting to know home students.

Reflection

Chiang appeared to be academically successful, well motivated and seemed to work hard. He had a lot of contacts but did not appear to have a close friend with whom he spent most of his time. Chiang had many friends on the campus but seemed to move around very independently (much like Pei and Xan). As with the other students, he appeared very independent and motivated, and his daily life was centred very much on the campus, library or computer rooms and classes.

Chiang had some interesting ideas about why he felt that it was not easy to get to know UK students. He believed that they had too much freedom and this meant that they were too 'naughty'. He appeared to have some preconceived ideas about other groups, ranging from those not from Shanghai to UK home students. In contrast to his views about home students being too free, he said that he enjoyed the extra freedom he had when he was abroad because when he was in China his parents were strict with him and he had to do as he was told. This was Chiang's first trip to a foreign country and he did not appear to display as many of the 'culturally aware' views of some of the other participants.

Sera

> I've got a really good mix of friends I have a lot of local English people, a few Irish friends, the majority would really be international students from all over really. I think I only really have one friend from my home country but that was what I had in mind when I came here. I didn't come to meet more Indians or home people from my own country. I was quite determined to meet people from the rest of the world so I didn't really go out seeking Indians.

Sera is a 24-year-old Indian female whose family are from Kerala in India, although her parents live in the Middle East. She is in the final semester of a Master's course in Art and Design. Like two of the other participants, Xan and Isken, she lived at the university campus, which was three miles from the city centre. Sera had a part-time job working for the university's student job shop and was quite heavily involved in the activities of the university Student Union, running for a post on the Student Union Executive and preparing election campaigns and publicity. She was also involved in the Student Union's International Society, where she held responsibility.

Sera's friends

Because of her involvement in the various societies, Sera had many contacts across the university. She was known to many of the international students at the university and nearly all of the students involved in this study had had contact with her. She had a smaller group of close friends, her closest being a female student from the Caribbean. She knew some British students and had made quite close relationships with the UK home students on her course. She talked about 'getting into the pub culture' and felt she had crossed this barrier and entered into the social life that was represented by 'the pub'.

She was a Christian and attended the local church in the city where she felt she had made some good friends with the local community, particularly of the older generation. Christianity was a factor in her close friendship with the student from the Caribbean, and she said that she felt that, despite their difference in nationality, they shared a common 'culture', and she believed this was to do with their religion.

Reflection

Sera appeared to be an extremely confident and socially successful person. She had become very involved in the social fabric of the university. She was very successful socially and was exceptional in the wide-ranging nature of her friendship group. Sera was certainly an example of a student who had managed to develop an extended and wide social network. Her links with Christianity and the church had also helped her network to extend beyond the university campus. She had developed quite strong working relationships with students on her course and she believed that these relationships had improved the quality of her university work. Her religious faith was very important to her, and she believed that the confidence and support she received from her religious group were a significant factor in her ability to succeed and to be able to carry on with her study.

Arin

> I am 28 and all those students [classmates] are 18. I am a mature student, in the complete sense of this word. I was used to travelling since I was a young kid; I actually travelled on my own to go to Poland. Yeah, I like to be independent, that's it. I couldn't do that in Italy...I guess I had to go abroad also to achieve my independence.

Arin is a 28-year-old Italian male from a small village near Milan. He is in his final year of a BA degree in Economics and has been in the UK for two years. Arin lived in the same accommodation as Pei, a university residence where many international students chose to live.

Arin's friends

Arin's closest friend at the university was Marcus, a Dutch male student, who was also a participant in this research. Arin also had a small but close group of friends who were in the Chess Club. He saw these students on a fairly regular basis and felt that they were amongst his closest friends. The members of the Chess Club group mainly lived at the campus three miles away from the city and they were part of the social network of that campus and often ate or shopped together. Arin missed out on this aspect of that group because he lived on the other side of the city in a self-contained flat.

Arin also had a group of UK home student friends from his course. These students were all male and he sometimes played football or went to the pub with them. He said he would have liked to get to know these students better, but their relationship remained rather superficial or 'erratic'. He thought this was because the UK students didn't attend lectures on a regular basis. He had a girlfriend, who was also a student from Denmark, and they spent a lot of time together. He believed that this was a kind of barrier to him having a wider set of friends.

Reflection

Arin said about himself that he was a mature student in all senses of this word, meaning in years but also in outlook. He felt that many of his classmates were quite immature and had a much more 'teenage' view on life. His relationships with them remained superficial, as he said they preferred to keep to superficial topics of conversation such as football, female students and beer. Although he said he sometimes liked to talk about these topics, he also said he sought more depth in his relationships. Despite his feeling of being more mature than his classmates I got the strong impression that he did not view them disdainfully, and from observation I found that he was well liked by his UK classmates.

Arin appeared to me to be a thoughtful and highly perceptive student who had advanced awareness of the differences which cultural and social diversity brings. He had lived in Iceland for two years before he came to study in the UK and he talked about the difficult acculturation process he experienced there. He felt his experiences in Iceland made it easier for him to settle quickly when he came to the UK as he had some previous experiences of being in a new culture and could draw upon these. Arin had Polish grandparents and had travelled to Poland as a young child for extended holidays. He had learned Polish but said he could not remember it. It may be that these family and linguistic factors are also aspects of his personal background which helped him to be socially confident and successful.

Marcus

> I tend to limit the very close contacts that I have to a very few number of people but I do, however, like a big group of friends who I know and like and call but I also give them a bit of distance...I tend to remember how important it is to know a lot of people.

Marcus is a 22-year-old Dutch male student in the second year of his BA in Economics and International Politics. He had been in the UK for two years and lived in a shared university flat on the city campus. A mix of nationalities from Europe and South East Asia shared his flat.

Marcus' friends
Marcus said that he knew a large number of students on campus and noted that he was able to get a large group of people together to participate in an activity. He said he preferred to have a big group of friends but even with these friends he said he kept them at 'a bit of distance'. He said 'I do tend to limit the very close contacts I have to a few people' and this appeared to be a deliberate and personal choice on his part. He made a point of emphasizing how useful friends can be to you. He said that this is one reason why he liked to get to know a wide range of friends, because you never know when you may need the help of someone in a particular academic or professional field. He had a girlfriend, who was German and studying in Europe, so they saw each other quite infrequently. Marcus said that he did not keep in touch that much with his friends and family back home, but did feel that he could contact them if he needed to. Of the people he had contact with at his university in the UK, he felt closest to his international friends, and, whilst he did know some UK home students, he did not feel particularly close to them.

Reflection
Marcus appeared to have some strong views about his relationships with others. He expressed a very functional view of his friendships, saying that he tended 'to remember how important it is to know a lot of people'. He was however, very sociable and enjoyed organizing social activities for groups of international students around the university. He also made a point of trying to remember the issues that these

acquaintances had in their lives and asking about any difficulties they had. As well as stating that his friends were useful, he said 'I really do like being amongst people.'

Marcus' attitudes to his UK classmates were quite negative. He saw them as uninterested in their academic subjects and he believed that their lack of interest in the course was something which somehow devalued the quality of his own educational experience. He viewed his home student classmates as being interested only in football and drinking, and frequently expressed the opinion that he felt he did not have the opportunity to discuss course-related and academic issues with them in the way that he believed he should. He said that he no longer tried to talk to his UK classmates about the course they were doing. He said he had tried, he felt without success, in the first three weeks to engage them in academic conversation but now did not even try to do so.

I found Marcus' views interesting and I felt that these views were living examples of stereotypes and their potential influence on social and academic interaction. Marcus' views about his classmates could form a barrier to positive and meaningful social and academic relationships.

Isken

> I hardly ever get depressed, but I usually comfort myself and if I have a problem I try at first to find a solution myself. Sometimes I do get depressed but what I do is I go and talk to my friends, other international friends. We are close so we can share the problem when we are on hard times. I love sharing that kind of problem, actually that gives me a feeling that there is somebody that understands me.

Isken is a 20-year-old Nepalese male completing the first year of his BA course in Health Development Studies and has been in the UK for almost a year. Isken is from a very small village in Nepal that has only 700 inhabitants. He is a member of a small ethnic group of Nepal and he is the first member of that ethnic community ever to come to university in the UK.

Isken's village is two days' walk from the nearest hospital and he said that many ill people died on their way there. Isken had lived in the village all his childhood and was educated in the village school which was funded by a UK charity foundation. He hoped to use what he learned at university in the UK to improve conditions back in his home environment. Whilst at university he lived in university residences three miles from the city centre.

Isken's friends

Isken had a wide group of friends and contacts both locally and across the UK. His education was sponsored by a UK charity and there were two families which oversaw his sponsorship and acted as guardians to Isken when he was at university abroad. He was quite close to these families, who lived in the South of England. In addition to this, Isken had a very strong international student friendship group, which was based at his university residences, and this group frequently cooked, ate and shopped together. The international student group in which Isken was involved also overlapped with Sera's group and Isken and Sera knew each other quite well, Sera's best friend (from the Caribbean) also being a close friend of Isken's.

Isken was the only international student on his course and had made contacts and good working relationships with his local UK classmates. Although Isken was only 20 years old, he found the younger UK students on his course a little immature and less well motivated than himself and he gravitated towards the mature female students in his group (and they to him), particularly when there was group work to be done. In general, Isken's friendship group was predominantly female and he said this was because he was the sort of person who likes to share his feelings with others. He said that this was not so easy with the UK males on his course.

Reflection

Isken appeared to me to be an exceptional student, enthusiastic and motivated. He was evidently popular and well known to his classmates and to groups of students around the campus.

Isken felt that he was privileged to be here in the UK and he appeared to like nearly everything about his situation at university abroad. He became involved in every aspect of the university experience that he possibly could and appeared to have achieved a very solid and extensive social network. It was impressive to consider that Isken was only 20 years old and he had already won awards for being an international student and had set up health and development projects in his own village in Nepal. He had travelled widely in Scandinavia and Europe and had a great interest in other countries and their cultures.

Isken, as himself, has written the postscript to this book. This account of his background illustrates the power of individual social and cultural backgrounds and their potential influence on education.

Student experience in context

Four contexts are described below to enable the reader to get a flavour of the experiences of the students. The first description is of the students at the bar, a place where relationships may be made and developed; the second and third contexts are the classroom, giving an interesting insight into the learning and teaching context; and the fourth is a longer description of the Chess Club, a Student Union society organized by international students and the focus for the development of supportive relationships.

At the pub with Arin

After a lecture one day Arin went to the pub with his home student friends. Well before lunchtime we went into a large, spacey, dark bar on campus. Arin met up with two home students, a male student from the North of England and another male student from Wales. It was Saint Patrick's Day so they were drinking pints of Guinness. Arin and I had halves of Guinness. The UK students said 'oh we're making him more English all the time but he still drinks halves', and they all laughed. We sat down at a table and they started chatting about beer. They had a long conversation about different types of Guinness, about Ireland and how beers are different between here and there. They compared beers in England and Italy and what we like to drink when we're 'abroad'. Arin then began to talk about football and classic Italian football players.

Arin was well integrated into the conversation, and although they talked in colloquial English he kept up with the conversation, despite the fast English and the cultural references such as 'bottle of dog' for a bottle of Brown Ale, a local drink. After about 20 minutes a third UK student joined the group. He had just got up and had missed the lectures. The other two UK students began explaining what he had missed and what the two lectures were about. They then talked about the exam and what was going to be in the exam, the three questions and what each question consisted of. They were supporting each other, discussing the academic content of the exam. Then one of the home students said 'we're having a session at J's house tonight to go over the questions'.

They then began to talk about a radio programme, which one of the home students had heard, about shortage subjects for degree graduates. One of the UK students said it would be great to finish the degree and be in demand internationally. One of the home students said he would love to work in Japan and another said he would really like to work in the Far East or South East Asia. I was struck by their optimism and expectations of an international future. They had a positive attitude to working abroad and to international careers. The boy who had just got up said he didn't want to be a 'bloke in a suit' though.

Then Marcus arrived in the bar and joined the group at the table. He seemed less well known to the home students and appeared quite nervous. He had obvious difficulty in getting into the conversation. Arin talked to him on the periphery of the group and made several attempts to bring Marcus into the group's conversation. Marcus remained on the edge of the group and talked only to Arin.

In class with Chiang

I went to class with Chiang. When we arrived Chiang chose a seat in the middle of the room. The UK home students were sitting round the sides in small groups, with the UK female students sitting together. The group was well mixed in nationality (including UK) and there was also a good mix of male and female students.

The lecturer was explaining some quite complex ideas about Freud and 'Western philosophy'. Chiang looked up a couple of words in his electronic dictionary. The lecturer asked students to talk about the questions he had set and stressed that students should work in mixed nationality groups. When the lecturer first asked the students to do this they all stayed in single nationality groups. The lecturer came round and said 'no, that's not what I said – mixed nationality!' and finally they moved into mixed groups.

Chiang was confident in speaking to the small group he was in (one male German student, one UK, and one Greek) and expressed his ideas fluently and well. They finished their question very quickly and the lecturer came and gave them another angle on a second question. Another group of four female students were having a lively discussion. The Greek student said to Chiang 'tell us about Jung, he must be Chinese'. Chiang said he didn't think he was Chinese but the Greek student insisted 'believe me, he must be Chinese, look at the spelling of his name!' The German student said 'I think he's German'. They all looked at me and said 'is he German or Chinese?' I said German but the students did not appear convinced by my answer. I found this an amusing international discussion. The lecturer came and solved the problem by saying 'yes, he's German'.

The group began to talk socially, as they considered they had completed the task. Chiang said to the German student 'Do you go to the gym now? I haven't seen you there for a long time'. The German student thought Chiang had said 'do you go to Germany?' but they sorted out the misunderstanding and laughed. Chiang asked about the German student's friend 'what about your friend – does he still go?' They obviously knew each other's immediate network. They were chatting in a very sociable way. Chiang confidently asked the other students in the group about what they were doing that weekend.

Then the lecturer brought the group together to answer the questions and feed back from their discussion. Chiang offered answers to the lecturer in front of the whole group and showed confidence in his answers. A UK female student offered an answer, but by her tone of voice she appeared unsure that what she was saying was right. The lecturer helped her, supported her ideas and restated and built on what she had said. The most confident of the Chinese female group gave an answer. Another Chinese female student tried to provide an answer but she was not heard. She stopped and didn't persevere.

There was an interesting discussion that involved all students, and all students in the group appeared to be engaged by the discussion. The international students had suddenly gained the confidence to speak in front of their peers, and in my opinion it was a result of the mixed nationality group work that preceded the plenary discussion which had built social relationships between the students.

In class with Isken

I went with Isken to one of his lectures. On this particular day it was a guest lecturer and the topic was Housing Policy. Isken was the only international student in this group, which was all female apart from Isken. The lecturer started off by trying to elicit information about housing policy, but no students offered ideas. She started to talk and asked questions and gradually students began to offer answers. She set a group work task and students began to discuss in groups of four. Isken said he couldn't hear properly and the younger UK female student explained what was being said. The group was talking about local authority housing (social housing provided by councils in the UK) and its advantages and disadvantages. The young UK student explained some unknown words to Isken, such as a 'bond'. He asked her when he didn't understand a word, but it was mainly cultural and contextual references that he found difficult.

After the discussion each group fed back and one student wrote up the answers. A lively discussion started between groups. Up to this point Isken had not offered any answers, although he was talking to the other students in the group. An interesting discussion ensued about council housing and antisocial behaviour. A number of students were living in council accommodation (government-funded housing) or had relatives living in social rented property, and this background (the socio-economic group of the students) appeared to be directing the discussion. Isken had no background or experience in this area.

In light of this it was interesting that Isken was chosen by his group to go and write up the answers on the whiteboard. One of the other groups said 'do you want another pen Isken?' The entire group knew his name and seemed to be trying to offer moral support and include him in the activity. The students returned to talking about council (government) properties and the laws relating to buying council-owned properties. Some students had a personal vested interest in this topic as they wanted to buy the houses they were living in themselves. I began to wonder how much of the discussion Isken was understanding and how it might be relevant to his learning.

Back in the group a student was explaining a problem she had on her own council estate relating to parking. She said her dad had a 'Merc'. They discussed parking problems where households have more than one car. Isken lived in a village where there were no cars.

Isken looked at the notes of the female student sitting next to him to try to work out the main points of the lecture. There was a huge amount of cultural background knowledge required; for example, the names of local housing projects were used without explanation. It was very interesting watching this class with knowledge of Isken's own particular social and cultural context. I had more of a perspective on this than the lecturer and most of the other students. I felt that the group had missed out on an opportunity for Isken to provide a very different perspective on the subject they were discussing.

The lecturer gave out some case studies for discussion. Isken was in a pair with another older female mature UK student. They discussed and made notes, working well together in a conscientious way. The female mature student (from a small town in the local area) explained some of the background to Isken. The two-person pair work was supportive to Isken as explanation was provided of cultural background information Isken did not have.

The Chess Club

> There are people I know on campus who are quite close to me... people at the chess club, I mean we don't meet that often but when we do meet we're looking after each other and you know I wouldn't mind sharing my problems with these people. (Arin)

The Chess Club is a Students' Union society set up by a small group of international students. An Indian student, Bridden, was the main organizer of the club and is only 19 years old but is in the final year of his degree in Accountancy. All the other students told me that he is a very intelligent person. The club met once a week and was a very informal arrangement where small groups of students turned up for a couple of hours and played each other at chess. There was a friendly but palpable sense of competitiveness between the members of the group.

During the time I spent with Arin and Xan I went to the chess club every week. Apart from being very enjoyable to play chess and talk to such a bright and interesting group of students, it provided an excellent opportunity to observe two students when they were relaxed and amongst a group of friends. This experience gave me a fascinating insight into the students' interaction with each other. This was the part of the observation where I was most personally involved, as I became an 'honorary' member of the club.

The small number of students in this group had clearly become very close to each other over the years that the club had been running. They enjoyed each other's company and all said that the club provided them with an opportunity to unwind but also to share difficulties or problems that they might have. Bridden appeared to be the central figure of the group and the other students clearly admired him. Xan said in his first interview that Bridden was his closest friend and that he would definitely go and talk to him if he had a problem or difficulty because he was 'wise', even though he was only 19 years old.

There was always a lot of talk at the club both during and between chess games. Topics of conversation ranged from international politics to discussing the lives of other members of the group (in other words gossip!).

I asked the group why they thought that only international students had joined their club. They said that they had had one UK male student join when the club first started but he only came twice. They also had a UK female student who came only once to the club. I asked why they thought they hadn't continued to come and Arin replied 'I think the students at this university are not interested in that sort of intellectual activity'.

The Chess Club was a fascinating discovery for me and it appeared to be quite a hidden activity, happening in a classroom tucked away in a quiet part of the university, with a small number of international students. Despite its unassuming nature, it was a core aspect of both Arin's and Xan's friendship groups. They both appeared to rely on the club as a means of support, taking the opportunity to share problems and difficulties with the various different students who were there in any given week. Because this Chess Club was such a good opportunity to study a network in more detail I decided to record a group discussion with the members of the club. This recording is integrated into the data of this book and referred to in a number of places across the following chapters.

Summary

This chapter has presented the friendships and social setting of the students who are part of this book. These portraits will enable the reader to put comments made by students in this book into their context, as the students presented in this chapter make an appearance throughout the following pages.

The vignettes of experience presented here speak for themselves as actual and recorded pictures of students' lives at a particular point. They have also raised some issues that may be more widely applicable or generalizable in terms of other students' experiences in similar contexts. For example, the influence of geographical aspects of students' experiences appears to be noticeable through the personal outlines presented in this chapter. Where students live in relation to the university, who they live alongside and who they spend time with appear to be strong factors in delineating their experiences. These geographical factors are also an influence on the ways in which they study in informal and social spaces.

In the case of the international students quoted in this book, being physically and geographically close on a particular campus or in particular accommodation gives them the opportunity to become close with other international students, to come together over food or in social spaces. Where these social spaces are not frequented by UK students the opportunity is not there for students to develop close and more profound relationships. Different student groups thus develop quite different geographical 'centres of gravity' (Shipton, 2005). This may not be an issue in the long run for international students, who meet and get to know students from many different countries, but may limit UK home students' opportunity to learn about diversity and to develop intercultural skills and competences (Deardorff, 2006).

The 'mechanics' of how, where and with whom students study thus exerts an influence on their perceptions of their learning experience. Previous research has suggested that this may in turn influence the outcomes of learning (Prosser and Trigwell, 1999). The social, functional and organizational aspects of students' learning experiences should thus be acknowledged as influential on their development.

It is also noticeable from the portraits of these students that some of them have other experience of living abroad prior to their arrival in the UK. Arin was born in Italy but has Polish parents and travelled to Poland as a child. He also lived in Iceland for two years before he came to the UK. Sera is from India but her parents live in the Middle East, and Isken has visited Scandinavia and other countries. These students all emphasized their desire to get to know a mixed international friendship group and saw the benefits of knowing people from other countries. This active interest in experiencing intercultural interaction and understanding what it means to experience more than one culture appeared to be significant in their positive approach to their opportunities to live and study in the UK.

In addition to this, the descriptions of students' experience present a picture of a teaching and learning environment that is not always positively disposed to interaction between different communities of students. It could be seen through the teaching session attended by Chiang, where the lecturer insisted on mixed groups of students, that the experience of social learning can be improved by approaches to group work. Whilst these may be simple techniques, they do require a social confidence and a willingness to take risks on the part of the lecturer, and a conviction that the decision to insist on multicultural learning environments will reap positive benefits.

4 International Student Networks: A Community of Practice?

This chapter suggests that international students form a strong international community that supports their learning and provides them with a supportive learning environment. Contrary to some perceptions that suggest that international students are isolated and wish to remain in single-nationality groups, the existence of a strong international community challenges this view, presenting a picture of a positive and supportive learning community that is an integral part of international students' social and academic resources. This strong social group could be viewed as a community of practice, with its shared aims and interests, its sense of history and initiation of new members.

Social networks and international students

'If you can make friends and if you have a deep need to make friends, you will be successful. It's people who can make a friend, who have friends, who can do well...' (Hall, 1998). An individual's social network consists of the patterned 'web' of their relationships with family, friends and other more distant acquaintances. Social networks and the support derived from these could be viewed as a 'resource' which is provided by this network of friends and acquaintances. Some studies suggest that a greater number of ties could increase health, happiness and even life-span (Walker et al., 1994). Similar individuals tend to form strong friendships, and network members tend to have similar characteristics, such as shared interests (Harrison and Peacock, 2007).

Particularly in the industrialized and 'developed' world, because of moves to find work, the immediate web of social life tends to consist less of stronger kinship ties and more of people whom we have met as a result of our move to develop careers. Relationships with families are often maintained at a distance and families are visited when work allows. Pilisuk and Hillier Parks point out:

> Our society recreates itself by escaping through travel and maintains commitments to relatives by an occasional uprooting trip for the holidays. (1986: 3)

For international students the result of their move away from home is similar to that experienced by many groups and individuals who have moved. The strong ties of kinship and family in the immediate context are exchanged for the weaker ties of acquaintances and new friendships.

However, distance is not necessarily an obstacle to close ties. In studies of North Americans it was found that their most intimate ties were distant ones. Physical access is not necessarily related to more important kinds of support, so that network members can provide support over large distances (Walker et al., 1994). This is of particular relevance to the study of international students who continue to receive support from family and friends who are geographically distant.

Social networks and modern technology

The development of technology has made it clear that social networks and communities are no longer necessarily local entities. Globalization has brought social and geographical mobility, and it is common for individuals and families to relocate both nationally and internationally for professional or educational reasons. This demographic instability has resulted in both friendship and kinship groups which are geographically dispersed. Modern technological communication means that distance is not necessarily a barrier to non-local friendships, and these can play an active part in people's lives. Modern technology has created new forms of primary group structure and family ties; neighbourhoods and friendships can be maintained despite breaks in face-to-face contact (Adams and Allan, 1998: 159).

In addition to email and the internet, mobile phones and text messaging appear to be a highly significant means for international students to communicate with friends and relatives, both locally and internationally. Whilst this use of technology is by no means exclusive to international students, it may be that a scarcity of local friendships is being compensated for by more reliance on distant networks, at least in the initial stages of their time abroad. Adams and Allan state:

> Online friendships supplement or sometimes are substitutes for offline relationships. Online networks thus affect the overall structure of people's friendship networks, either by being added to them or by changing the offline relationships themselves. (1998: 171)

It may be that international students' reliance on friendship networks that are maintained by means of technology may become a distraction from developing offline networks in their 'real' context. Adams and Allan (1998) emphasize that insufficient empirical research has been carried out on online friendship networks, particularly in respect of density, size and solidarity. However, the idea of technology as a support to friendship and kinship is an interesting one, as it touches on the idea of a global community that is maintained despite geographical distance.

Social capital and international students

Bourdieu (1985) produced a series of studies throughout the 1970s and 1980s in which he expanded the notion of capital beyond its economic conception, which emphasizes material exchanges, to include immaterial and non-economic forms of capital, such as cultural and symbolic resources. Bourdieu considered social capital to include language, cultural knowledge and credentials, including education. Cultural capital represents the collection of non-economic forces such as family background, social class, varying investments in and commitments to education and other resources that could influence academic success (Coleman, 2000).

So membership of social networks, or social capital, is a means of acquiring advantage both socially and educationally. When groups of individuals share the same values, ideas and strength of cooperation they can access advantages provided by their network as part of their social capital. But group solidarity in communities is frequently accompanied by hostility towards 'out-group' members. There appears to be a natural human tendency to categorize the world into friends and enemies (Fukuyama, 1999). So the strength provided by social capital or social network may have a negative effect when individuals are not included, as they are viewed as the outsider, 'the other' or the one who is different.

It is interesting, then, to consider how the issue of social capital has an influence on the relationships that international students form in their experience in Higher Education. When a person moves to a new social context that is geographically or socially distant from their own, there is a sense in which they are separated from access to their own resources of social capital. They can no longer draw upon their friends, acquaintances and family, their social network, to access support or advantage in the same way as before. Even if they are from an advantaged or elite background in their home country, once they arrive in their new context international students lose their social advantage, as they are in a totally new social context where they are not linked in to relationships that carry social advantage. They do not have access to the power that accompanies some forms of social capital.

In their home contexts international students may have been in professional or social positions that commanded considerable social capital. Postgraduate students may have worked in businesses where they were managers or, in the case of some PhD students, they may have been teachers at high levels in universities in their home countries. These positions are associated with respect and power and access to social capital in these cases would have been great.

The data from the research project that supports this book indicates that international students develop very purposeful and functional relationships. Their approach to friendship associates value with friends who can help them and support them both in their studies and in their lives at university and beyond. It may be that home students feel the same way about their friendships. There is a strong sense in which, if international students have little access to social capital which would benefit the home student, then it would be difficult to reciprocate the relationships practically with help, be it social, academic or emotional. In this case it may not appear to be useful for home students to form friendships with international students. On the other hand, international students to a certain extent share the same goals as students from other international countries, sharing interests and having much in common. Because of this they are able to offer each other social capital and access to support and social and educational resources.

The theory of social capital provides an empirically established relationship between membership of social networks and educational achievement. This gives support to the idea that international students' social capital, in the form of their social networks, could affect their educational and personal attainment and ultimately their learning. These important social networks extend further than the geographical boundaries of the university, yet may still influence the learning experience.

International students in a community of practice

The development of social networks and social capital is linked with the idea of communities of practice. A community of practice is a group of people who share concerns, problems and interest in a particular topic and who develop their knowledge on this particular topic by interacting with each other (Wenger et al., 2002). Communities of practice are supportive and purposeful in nature, a complex combination of purposeful social activity and the group's construction of their own idea of themselves. In some cases it may be that a purposeful community of practice may be a means of developing social capital. As a community of practice is developed, so a social network emerges, and this developed network may form a resource through which social capital can be developed or rebuilt.

Lave and Wenger developed an 'apprenticeship' model of learning where learners are viewed as cognitive apprentices who begin their learning process on the periphery of a given group. Their initial position at the edge of the community is seen to be 'legitimate' and in keeping with the early stages of their learning. As their learning and understanding develop they move closer towards the 'centre' or expert positions of the learning community in which they are participating. A community of practice changes over time, through history and culture, and an aspect of the apprenticeship model is that the community has longer-standing participants who act as experts or old-time guides to the newer apprentice participants. In other words, the existing members of the group support and help the newcomers to learn to 'be' in the community.

As will be seen in the following discussions in this chapter, there are many senses in which the international student group studied here forms a community of practice. They share goals and values, provide support for each other and develop a particular group identity that evolves over time as students learn about each other, about their new context and about the nature of Higher Education.

A supportive and purposeful friendship group: A community of practice?

The international students in this research talk extensively about how they provide support for their friends. There is a strong sense that they are always willing and happy to help their friends and that they are active in supporting their contacts when they have difficulties. One of the students attending the Chess Club, when asked whether he provided support for his friends, replies:

> Yeah. Well I mean people I know I ask them how things are going and I mean some people might treat that as a formality and say I'm fine and nothing's happening but other people if they truly want to let me know, they would tell me what's happening and you know I just share with them what they're experiencing and if they do have problems I'm always going to help, always going to help.

Students also note that they support each other with the practical aspects of their academic work. The tasks they help each other with are various and include handing in assignments, help with proofreading, and discussing aspects of their work with others. Pei, the Chinese female student, says that if she has to miss a class she can rely on her friends not only to look after her but also to collect handouts for her.

> And also when I was ill they could stay with me and the others could bring some handouts [from] the course.

In addition to this willingness to help with general issues and difficulties, there is a strong sense of academic support for each other within this international student group. Xan, the Indonesian male student, relies on friends to keep him up to date with notes, but he is also part of groups set up to discuss academic work and exchange information. He says:

> [I work or study] mostly with the Greek girl off my course. If I missed the lecture or she missed the lecture I would get materials or notes for her. We [had] some discussion for example for a group assignment we exchanged some information or gave ideas. Like helping each other with study, yeah.

Pei describes well-organized study skills groups:

> Mainly we are talking about the study because sometimes in class we don't understand the lectures and some friends will email me to say they have some questions. Then we will arrange a meeting and talk about the lecture. So we have study groups, normally in the library.

A deliberate choice of friends and purposeful contacts made with other students are also noticeable in the social networks of this group of students. Xan interprets the behaviour of one of his friends as not being conducive to achieving high grades in exams and assessments, and therefore he chooses not to discuss academic work with him but to select friends for this who can help him achieve his aims.

> Q. Did you tend to get into groups with him [his friend] for discussion and so on?
>
> A. [With] the Greek girl yes but with Mark to be honest no because it seems like he is failing his course. So usually we don't discuss with him. From my point of view I'm better with the other students. I can get better marks you know.

This appears to be quite a functional approach to friendship, and Xan has formed friendships with a view to ensuring the best personal outcome for himself.

Arin, the male Italian student, is also conscious of the purposeful and useful nature of his friendship with his close friend Marcus, the male Dutch student, and feels that they both benefit from the academic support they provide for each other. He says:

> Well I've got quite a partnership with Marcus, we study together to prepare for exams, I help him and he helps me. Yeah I think we're getting a great deal out of this friendship.

These practical and academic aspects of support are considered important by students and appear to be one of the factors that help them to function effectively in their new environment. The combination of psychological encouragement and practical, academic help seems to be a significant factor in what helps these international students to continue with their lives in a new country. In this sense students could be viewed as building social capital through the activities of their social network (Milroy and Gordon, 2003). In addition to this, a social network is a valued aspect of their academic experience and in some ways enriches their learning process. Isken, the Nepalese male student, notes:

> It's quite nice also discussing things with a friend. If I really want to decide if I have understood the course alright then when we are talking we definitely see the reflections of our knowledge that we have gained in the class.

There are aspects of reciprocity and functionality in the students' relationships that recur throughout the research, and these appear to be particularly applicable to the international student group and do not appear to extend to the home student group. Arin indicates that he does provide support for the UK home students he knows to some extent, but that this is not reciprocated. Academic exchange does not appear to happen with these home students in the same way as it does with his international student contacts. Arin claims that his home student friends are less engaged with the course than he is and are erratic in their class attendance. Because of this their relationship remains on a superficial level. He says:

> Well emotionally it's nice for me to hang out with them, we have a laugh you know and talk about football and girls. I like that but with information level I don't think they help me.
>
> Q. Even though they're on your course?
> A. Actually the thing is I give them some information about the course as they don't come so often.
> Q. So they're more likely to ask you?
> A. Yes, it's more likely that I know about something than they do.

Xan has also provided academic help for a range of his contacts and friends, including home students. This was because in his first semester he received the highest marks in the group and therefore he was asked for help by other students.

Xan is accomplished academically and because of this is in a position to support his friends. This picture of international students being givers of information, sometimes gaining the highest mark in their class and being a source of knowledge and academic support for others, runs contrary to the anecdotal perception of the international student as requiring support and being deficient in study skills, language and background knowledge. In this respect the data here contrasts with the deficit model of the international student, presenting a much more positive image of the skills and abilities of these students. It suggests that international students play an active rather than a passive role in the student learning community.

A community with a sense of time and history: A community of practice?

The research suggests that students help and support their contacts by passing on information and experience which they have gained themselves. There is an informal initiation of newcomers to the group, carried out to spare the new students the difficulties experienced by their friends. This further aspect of the way that the international group appears to be forming a strong community is an indication that their network could be regarded as a community of practice. When asked if she feels she supports others, Sera, the Indian female student, says:

> I think I do yes because of the experience I got when I first came here, when I look at a new person I can almost feel what they're thinking about 'oh I feel lost and that everyone is unfriendly'. So I sort of bring this up in conversations and say this is what I felt I felt the same as you but later I realised that some people are friendly just give a bit of time.

This sense of empathy with new students appears to be an important aspect of the forming of a strong bond amongst the international student group. In this sense the group has a sense of time and history, as students talk about relying on information and support from students who have been here for longer than themselves and the ways that experience is passed on to help those who have recently arrived. Arin says:

> If I have [had] a serious problem, I have spoken to Bridden. You know, just to get his opinion he's been living longer in the UK.

Xan expresses a similar view when he talks about his closest friend and the fact that he has already been here for a year. He says:

> Yeah the Indian guy who was at the Chess Club, he was last year's student as well. He stayed here last year as well. He is my closest friend.

Isken, the Nepalese student, also interprets his situation as being one in which he can learn from the difficulties past students in his current group have had and from this improve his own experience. He says:

> We can learn by observing and meeting international friends and ask them what they have done so far. We can learn from each others' mistakes, from my friends' experience.

Finally, throughout the data the strong sense of group and identity amongst the international students comes through. Isken says:

> Actually, when we come here the first thing we remember is that all of us are the international students and the problems we are facing are all similar. Some

> like me myself have been quite good at coping with the different cultures and different environments but they do have concerns as well. We always feel we are the international students and we must help each other.

Thus, the overall impression formed by this data is that the international student group is a strong and well-defined supportive entity which helps students to carry on in their lives at university.

Learning in the community of practice

The research also indicated that the students in this group use their friendships to support their study and learning. The learning focused upon here is a social aspect of learning and is twofold. First, there is the 'academic' learning of the classroom, which has an indirect link with the international students' social networks through group work and supportive relationships with classmates. Second, there is a sense of learning about oneself and others and developing communication skills that comes about through involvement in the social network. These two social aspects of learning are often difficult to separate from each other.

Through discussion of their assignments and proofreading of each other's work, the international students benefit from the knowledge and skills that their friends can bring. Indeed, this social aspect of learning becomes an important part of their learning experience in itself and provides a sort of added value. Isken in particular notes this and indicates that the learning that he experiences in terms of his relationships with his international student network is a valued part of his learning experience at university.

Summary

The international students in this study were participants in supportive social networks, which did not substantially include home students but which nevertheless assisted them in practical ways to cope with daily life as a student, helping them towards academic success. One question is whether we should regard this as an adjunct to the 'real' learning of their academic subjects or a part of it. The research shows that 'other' learning was taking place in addition to the acquisition of subject knowledge. This was learning about how to live in a new context, which was perhaps a springboard for learning about oneself and about other people. Indeed, it could be said that the international students' experiences of living abroad had exerted a powerful influence on them. Ullman (1998) notes:

> The act of immigrating to a new country can profoundly affect a person's social identity. In fact, some people experience this change more as an act of recreation than as a temporary period of readjustment.... These transformations are complex and continual, redefining all aspects of self.... (1998: 1)

The concept of a 'community of practice' (Lave and Wenger, 1991) is interesting and useful in this discussion because it promotes a view of learning that sees the participation in sociocultural activities as central to the learning process. Lave and Wenger see learning as a 'situated activity' and one in which learners acquire knowledge and skills through their participation in communities. Indeed, in order to acquire knowledge and skills, learners must move from 'legitimate peripheral participation' (1991: 29) towards full participation in the social and cultural practices of the community. The movement towards full participation is supported by other members of the community of practice, and previous knowledge and experience is passed between 'old-timers' and 'newcomers'. Thus a shared identity evolves and learning is given a meaning by this process of becoming a full participant in a sociocultural practice. As Lave and Wenger note:

> This social process includes, indeed it subsumes, the learning of knowledgeable skills. (1991: 29)

The students in this study share the common goal and primary purpose of academic success. They learn how to be successful students and within this context individually address their diverse range of academic subjects. They support each other emotionally and academically. Information and experience is passed from student to student. The group members are purposeful in their choice of friends, and being successful in their studies is of prime importance. At times friendship is a significant support. Their group has a sense of time and history, and experience is passed on to support those who are newly arrived and are just joining the group. There seems to be a perception within this strong group that one of the factors in its development is the sharing of experiences, and this makes friendship closer. There is also the feeling that there is always a common topic of conversation in the shape of shared experience, and this engenders closer and more supportive relationships. This functional and close group appears to be similar in nature to a community of practice as defined by Lave and Wenger.

The combination of psychological encouragement and practical, academic help provided by the group is a significant factor in the learning experiences of these international students. In addition to this, it is viewed as a valued aspect of their academic experience and one that enriches their learning process. Indeed, if the theory of the community of practice is applied to the students in this study, it can be said that the students' social activity is an integral part of their learning experience. Although the most obvious purpose of the community of practice is learning how to be academically successful, students are also learning something else through their participation. This could be considered to be an aspect of preparation for living and working in a global community. The data supports the assertion that the international students had the sense that they had changed because of their experience at university abroad. Arin talked about his sense that he had become more able to get on with anyone, and Xan talked about a similar feeling that he could adapt his own communication to suit a very wide range of different groups or 'cultures'.

So it seems that the strong social group formed by the students in this study demonstrates characteristics of a community of practice, with its shared aims and interests, its sense of history and initiation of new members. One of the purposes of this community of practice appears to be the reconstruction of the social capital that the students lose through their transition to a new context. The social resources that supported them in their home environment are replaced by a network of international students who share a powerful motivation to succeed and who support each other academically, socially and to a certain extent emotionally.

Wenger (1998) points out that our HE institutions approach learning as if it were an individual process, focused on subject knowledge and skills, and occurring as a direct result of teaching. Wenger's theories of communities of practice emphasize 'participation' as learners become active participants in 'the practices of social communities and constructing identities in relation to these communities' (1998: 4). In the community of practice of international students we can see social and intellectual interchange supporting academic success whilst the community also promotes the development of new identities as part of a global community. We can therefore challenge the assumption that international students are losing out if they do not 'integrate' with home students.

5 International Students and Home Students: Worlds Apart?

A major challenge for students in university life can come from friendships and relationships with new people whose backgrounds, experiences, goals and desires are different from their own. Encountering diversity can be threatening and unsettling and can pose threats to students' sense of who they are (Jackson, 2003). Experiences of diversity and social and cultural difference can also be a catalyst for positive change.

This chapter discusses the friendships of international students and home students and considers how the nature of these relationships may influence students' experience of Higher Education. It is suggested that there are strong underlying factors in the learning environment that appear to have an impact on relationships between international and home students, and these include differing motivations and attitudes to university and to social life and a difference in the geography of students' experiences, with varied centres of gravity of where students spend their time. Research from the study that supports this book shows that, whilst international and home students do form relationships, these bonds are more superficial and peripheral than the relationships across the international student group.

Amongst other research relating to international and home students' friendships, this chapter describes the convergence of two research projects. One project is the research around which this book is based, focusing on the social networks of international students and their effect on the learning experience. The other explores the development of younger home students' sense of 'self' as it develops through the course of their experience at university.

Initial findings in these projects give an insight into the perceptions of these two groups of students, illuminating issues of friendship, independence and development of 'self'. Whilst it is not intended to directly compare these two projects, as they were carried out separately and with different research aims and foci, this chapter presents some of the findings of these two research projects as their examination provides a wide-ranging perspective on the social experience of students in Higher Education.

The experience of young UK students: The Shipton study

A study of the perceptions of young undergraduate students was carried out by Shipton (2005) at the same UK university where this book's main study of international students was conducted. Shipton's study focused on the home student experience and the resulting impact of that experience on an awareness of 'self'. Forty interviews with 10 students at different stages of their university careers were conducted. During the interviews participants were invited to tell the story of how they came to the university and recount their experience since they arrived.

The study found that the personal development of these young undergraduate home students appeared to take place separately from the content of Higher Education. The perception of the students was that their academic programmes appeared simple, unengaging and straightforward, and this seemed to be in contrast to the complexity and ambiguity in the learning embedded in social practices. In other words, the home students in the Shipton study appeared to be very much concerned with aligning themselves with a distinct social group and this, rather than any academic or professional motivations, seemed to be their driving force. One of the students in the study said:

> The main reason you stay is not because of the degree, it's what's attached to it. It's the experience of meeting friends, the personal development, it's that that keeps you ... yes, I'd say for 85 per cent of people, that keeps you at university. (Shipton, 2005: 130)

It appeared that the students in the study felt a very strong need to share their experience with others in a particular social group in order to establish a 'sense of self'. One of them stated:

> Everybody just gets into these little groups and that little group is their identity, it can dictate what you do. (Shipton, 2005: 45)

The students seemed to continually classify themselves and others, using resources and discourse provided by youth culture, such as the labels utilized in the areas of music, sport, clothes and leisure activities (Mills, 2000). Thus, youth culture groups such as 'Trendy', 'Ras' and 'Homebirds', not the academic context of their university course, formed the significant context to the young undergraduate home student experience.

In some cases there was a sense that participation in these groups was constricting and prevented students from socializing outside their particular social group. There was a sense from some students that in the early stages of their course they were trapped within these social groups and this engendered a sense of loneliness. One of the students noted:

> There is a lot of isolation at university, people don't realise it, you think "Oh yeah, I'm going to meet people" but it's kind of hard to cross-breed out of those cells. You know you can't jump out of these cells. I think it's just the way society is. You just have to conform. (Shipton, 2005: 45)

In the Shipton study, the 'quest' to find a social group appeared to be part of a fear of isolation and insecurity in students' sense of who they were. One home student said:

> You are alienated in the environment, you don't know what to do. You lose all kinds of confidence. When you do realise what you are inside is actually ok is when it's on the outside. But you've got to try it out to be respected...you only know who you are by other people's reactions to you. (Shipton, 2005: 116)

Shipton perceived there to be loneliness and isolation in the young students' experience. He tells of one student's attempts to engage with fellow home students being met with defensiveness and mistrust. The student stated:

> Sometimes nothing seems to be the best option. I try to be friendly but am just met with "Hi"...no real interest...I am fed up trying to make an effort, they just don't know me. (Shipton, 2005: 118)

These comments have interesting resonances with the feelings of international students in their attempts to get to know home students. In addition to this, the views presented above suggest that home students feel constrained by their social groups and at times isolated within the university environment. They appear to experience alienation and feelings of rejection by other social groups much in the same way that international students do. This could be an underlying factor in the limited contact between home and international students.

For the home students in the Shipton study, their reasons for going to university stemmed mainly from the fact that everyone else in their final year at school was going so it was 'a natural progression'; they went with the crowd and drifted into Higher Education. One student said:

> It's no big deal, really there is little choice. You either go to a job and be told what to do, or go to university. (Shipton, 2005: 42)

They perceived university life, as presented in the media, to be a phase with few constraints, a euphoric and indulgent chapter of your life where you can bond with others and have fun.

In addition to this, part-time work and life away from campus was the students' 'centre of gravity' and university work was like a 'dark shadow' that followed them in their pursuit of 'having a laugh', actually a complex phenomenon, according to the Shipton study, and one that was significant in students' establishing a 'viable sense of self' (2005: 107).

Shipton found little sense of students feeling that they were being inducted into an academic discipline, although by the final year students' working on dissertations usually resulted in greater engagement and awareness of learning. The students in this study felt that there was a balance between socializing and study, but most of the students participating in this study said they would opt for 'fun' and a 2.2, rather than less 'fun' and a 2.1.

Shipton also noted an emphasis on a strategic approach sometimes centred on assessment requirements and a sense that students felt that some lecturers' approaches to teaching encouraged this. Shipton found it interesting and surprising that the young undergraduate home students implied that achievement orientation was encouraged in learning and that students felt that they were being encouraged to simply comply with the 'prescriptions' of course requirements, which they felt were onerous rather than engaging. Shipton noted that the following student comment was typical of their views:

> They are always going on about assessment. It's assessment, assessment, assessment. They seem to panic over it. (2005: 121)

One student expressed his detachment from his academic work and from his tutor as follows:

> The lecturer gets through it as fast as he can, you just go and do it, pass it and then it's like for the rest of your life, you just plan it out and do it. (Shipton, 2005: 98)

Another student makes it clear that he feels a passive audience to the content of his course and also feels that he himself is not valued. He said:

> First year experience – you just listen to the lecturer, with emphasis on listen, I mean there is too much talking and you just sit there and then you bugger off. (Shipton, 2005: 98)

Academic work appeared to the young home students to be ordered, regulated, rational, in contrast to their student experience being chaotic, full of desires, scandals and gossip. In contrast to their attitudes to study, for these students, part-time work provided a sense of stability and distracted students from the 'dark shadow' of study (ibid.)

Despite this picture of disengagement and alienation from university study and an 'obsession' with development of identities and selves, Shipton noted a development over the course of the three years of the young UK students' undergraduate study. When they reached their final year it appeared that students had begun to value differences and similarities in the student group that surrounded them. It appeared that by this final stage of their time at university they were able to appreciate the value of 'otherness' and they were released from their preoccupation with image, having developed a confidence in themselves. Shipton associated this development in many cases with the development of professional identities and an emerging awareness that they must change to 'fit in with the outside world'. Shipton notes:

> I sensed that a "sense of self" had evolved as a result of interrelating, which led to flexibility and a new capacity to communicate. (Shipton, 2005: 71)

This emergent ability to communicate is similar to the intercultural communication described by the international students in the study that supports this book.

The significance of the Shipton study in terms of resonances with the international study of this book is that the home students in his study appeared to have some motivations and priorities in their university life that may differ from those of international students. The young undergraduate home students studied by Shipton appeared to have drifted into Higher Education as part of a predetermined life course. Their friends in the sixth form were going and it was generally expected that they would go too. In this sense these students appeared to be passive in their choice to go into Higher Education. To contrast this with the international group in this study, more than one student talks about coming into Higher Education in the UK as being part of a 'childhood dream'. So there are aspects of the Shipton study that indicate a different 'centre of gravity' in the social lives and motivations of international and home students.

Understanding home students' perception of international students

Research carried out by Harrison and Peacock (2007) sought to show the perspective of home students on international students' participation in Higher Education. Their study canvassed the views of home students on Arts and Business courses where the proportion of international students ranged from 10% to 50%. Participants came from a range of ages and ethnicities within the home student group.

Home students in the Harrison and Peacock study stated that they had experienced only limited interaction with international students. There was a tendency in their accounts to associate similarity with friendship (and this has echoes in the Shipton study) and to assume that difference was a barrier to the development of relationships. For example, difference in age was a factor that recurred as a perceived obstacle to extended social interaction with international students, and interestingly this is an issue that was also perceived to be prominent for the international students. Discourse about the international students was very general and specific interests, names or actual countries of origin were not known; they were perceived to be 'shy', 'introverted' or 'difficult to get to know' (2007: 4).

The most significant barrier to interaction reported by the home students in the Harrison and Peacock study was language skills and use. However, this was not as straightforward as it may seem. The students in the Harrison and Peacock study noted that international students with poor language ability required more effort to get to know, and there were also anxieties around fears of being misunderstood, with negative experiences in this area being a source of discouragement to try to talk again (ibid.). The students felt that conversations with international students required 'mindfulness' and they were unwilling to make the effort as they 'just wanted to relax and have a laugh' (2007: 5). Indeed where international students' language proficiency was greater there were other significant barriers that emerged, in particular the ability to 'have a laugh' and the importance of 'getting it'.

However, the complexities and variation in perceptions and responses to international students were also underlined in the Harrison and Peacock study, with the home students noting variety in behaviour and participation within nationality. The home students pointed out that some international students fitted the stereotypes of being motivated and hardworking but that others did not fit with this picture. Interestingly, the researchers on the project felt that during the focus groups with home students there was a need to first explore the stereotypes of international students before they paradoxically concluded that there was considerable variation and they were simply more comfortable with students who shared the same work orientations and extroversions regardless of cultural backgrounds (Harrison and Peacock, 2007).

The friendships of international students

This part of the chapter provides a description of the friendship groups of the participants in the international research project and presents quotes from international student interviews that illustrate their relationships with home students.

A mixture of nationalities and a large friendship group

Students described their friendship groups as being made up of a mixture of nationalities. Sera indicates that she has a good mixture of nationalities in her friendship group. But the range of nationalities is what she terms 'international' as opposed to UK. She says that she has some UK friends but that she has mainly international friends. She says:

> I've got a really good mix of friends. I have a lot of local English people, a few Irish friends, the majority would really be international students from all over

> really. A lot of my close friends are from Europe, France, Germany and Spain and all those places. Some very good close friends are from the Caribbean.

This mixture of nationalities is mirrored in the social group described by Marcus; he describes a predominantly international group with some UK friends. He says:

> I've been here now for six months. I do have some UK friends but the majority of my friends are from abroad. That can range from the UK, EU then Asia and South America so there is a broad variety in the friends that I have.

Students also describe their friendship group as being a large group. In some cases this large group is familiar with each other and Xan says that they 'get on well'. Marcus also describes his friendship group as being extensive; he is active in organizing group games and activities and feels that this is testament to the large group of contacts he has. He says:

> I organise a lot of activities like watching football matches together or [going] bowling and then it is remarkable how many people I can get together.

This is also supported by Isken's perception of the size of his group of friends. He feels he knows a lot of people in the UK and many of these links have originated from contacts in his home country.

A close relationship of your own nationality: An emotional anchor?

Of these large numbers of friends, Xan, Chiang, Pei, Marcus and Sera all report that they have one or two friends in particular who are close or closer than the others. These closer friends often appear to be of the same nationality. Xan reports that of his mixture of international friends the closest are those from the Indonesian society (his own nationality). They are close with these people despite the fact that they did not know each other before they travelled abroad. Xan says:

> Yes in the city [campus] [there are] about the same number of people in the group but they are Indonesian students. So we are very close from the Indonesian Society ... I came here with a group of 15 students but I met them only at the airport so we were all brought by the same agency so they just booked a ticket for all of us and we came to England on the same plane.

It is interesting to note the almost arbitrary nature of their close friendships with their own nationalities and interesting to conjecture whether these people would become friends in their home country. Their friendship develops in their new context perhaps because they have much in common and they are thrown together in a sometimes difficult new situation.

Both Chiang and Marcus say that they have at least one close friend of their own nationality. Sera also indicates that, whilst she did not want to spend time with friends of her own nationality, she felt that having contact with people from her own nationality was important. She says:

> I think I only really have one friend from my home country but that was what I had in mind when I came here. I didn't come to meet more Indians or home people from my own country. I was quite determined to meet people from the rest of the world so I didn't really go out seeking Indians. Apart from one or two who I clicked with because you do need to have someone from your own country; that is good. I didn't really want to hang out too much with them because I wanted to make sure that I meet lots of other people.

Pei also indicated this deliberate intention to develop an international friendship group. She considered herself to be different from her close friends in that she has a desire to extend her friendship group. She thought that her friends of her own nationality need the security of other Chinese friends more than she did. She says:

> Yes, compared to Cynthia, Sophia, Carol and Meredith I think I am [an] outgoing person. I'd like to get to know more people. Sometimes I ask them would you like to go out with me to somewhere else like that we don't know. They will say no we have some other things to do. They are really very shy ... some of them said that if we didn't go would you go? I said yes I will. Even [though] they asked me 'no don't go', it didn't matter I [would] still go.

Being of the same nationality does not mean that one has the same attitudes to being with others, as individual and personal characteristics matter much more. This story also indicates that Pei had to take a risk in the social sense in order to widen her friendship group.

A hierarchy in choice of friends?

One student, Chiang, a male student from China, expresses ideas about choice of friends. He indicates that he has a hierarchy in his choice of friends. Chiang indicates that his first choice is to make friends with international students and then he prefers to make friends with UK students and lastly students from his own city. He says:

> First [I make friends with] international students, British students and students from Shanghai ... but if it's a Chinese friend I make I prefer to make friends from the same city as me like Shanghai.

Chiang recognizes that this could be seen as discrimination but he says that this is simply what is done in China for reasons of class and also pressure from parents; people from Shanghai tend to associate mostly with others from the same city. He says:

> We have, I don't know whether its like discrimination but Shanghai is a highly developed city and very many Chinese there, we are posh Chinese and so sometimes we just discriminate some people from other parts of China. For me maybe I do have some of these ideas and my parents also don't like me to make friends with other Chinese because it's no help for me for my language, for my future.

Thus both Chiang and his parents view his choice of friends as being significant in his future. His friends are part of his development and education. However, there is an aspect of this comment that could be seen as prejudiced. Preconceived ideas about home students could affect students' choice of friendship groups. The preference for forming relationships with other international students could be based on a set concept of how home students are. On the other hand, there may be experiences which underpin these impressions. Chiang says:

> And many friends from other countries like British students, some of them are not particularly friendly and they always get together with other British students. It's not easy to get into their community so I try my best to make friends with international students.

There is a certain irony in this comment as the accusation of preferring to stay with one's own nationality is often levelled at international students. Chiang obviously perceives this to be a trait of home students. It appears in the light of the Harrison and Peacock study quoted above that there are misconceptions on both sides.

International students' friendships with home students

As far as 'successful' relationships with home students are concerned, the international students, like the home students in the Harrison and Peacock (2007) study, appeared to believe that there were certain barriers to the success of these particular contacts. Arin considered that lack of opportunity to spend extended periods of time with home students is a significant factor in their failure to properly develop friendships, although Arin is one of the students in the study who reports some success with his home student counterparts. He does believe that there is the potential at least for these relationships to flourish. He says:

> Yes I think I have made a positive impact on their [home students'] lives. I think that they like me and I like them. That's good. But the relationship isn't very deep yet because there's this problem that they do not attend as often as they should so that is probably the main factor of limiting the degree of the relationship. Potentially we could be good close friends in the future, next year.

However, there is a recurring sense that there are some prejudgements on the part of the international students which affect their openness to the home students whom they come into contact with. The stereotype of the British as being 'reserved' is quoted by Arin as being another reason that it is difficult to get to know home students. Expanding on this, he feels that if another person makes the first move towards being friendly with home students then there is the potential to get to know them better. There appears to Arin to be a lack of effort on their part and a sense that home students are holding back until someone else makes that effort. During the Chess Club discussion, Arin says:

> I mean generally British people are more reserved, generally anyway. I mean you have exceptions obviously and I have noticed that they don't really make an effort unless you make an effort. And when you do make that effort it's like they're reacting to what you're saying. I mean maybe they truly are open to new people but they just don't make the effort to go and be upfront. Sometimes they just, they're just waiting for somebody else to come up to them.

The issue of who 'has to' make the first move towards breaking down barriers is an interesting one, since each side may be waiting for the other to do this.

In addition to Arin's views on the 'reserved' nature of the British, the social life associated with the pub and drinking is again seen to be an issue. This may be another psychological barrier for international students; the idea of the pub and drinking is often perceived to be a major obstacle. The phenomenon of drinking heavily is seen by Arin to be a 'Northern European' pattern of behaviour and one which is designed to encourage people to become more sociable and friendly. Arin offers interpretations about culture in Northern Europe when he says:

> Well this is a general phenomenon that is going on in Northern Europe. It's also a cultural thing; if you get drunk [in some cultures] it's a bit of a shame. But in Northern Europe I think people actually get drunk in order to become more sociable.

Arin, like Sera, also believes that going to the pub is a prerequisite if more sociable relationships are to be developed with home students. He believes that if you approach this with moderation then it won't be a problem, although his friend in the Chess Club points out that some people do use the pub to socialize but others go simply with the intention of getting drunk.

> And it's the pub as well. You know I mean if you need the social life with them you'd have to go to a pub but you don't have to drink, obviously. You'd have to be prepared to do that if you want to socialise with British students. I mean it's only in moderation, it's not like you have to get drunk or anything.

Having said that there is negative feeling in the relationships between international students and their home student counterparts, there is at the same time evidence of useful and positive academic and intellectual exchange occurring. Isken talks about his discussion and exchanges with his classmates on one of his courses in the most positive way and interprets this activity as being important and significant in his learning experience. He talks about what he has contributed to class discussions as a result of his background and how he has provided a different angle on topics discussed in class. He is the only international student on his course and it seems that being the only international student could be perceived quite differently (from both the international and home student points of view) than where there are larger groups of international students. Isken says:

> I did contribute regarding something about the Third World and how people are living there and what their problems are. I have learned from the mature

> [UK] students. What they [UK students] are contributing is really interesting and it is like just sharing information which is really important actually. Outside of our lecture we talk about every type of thing, about life, about the world problems. I used to say tell me about the health system in your country. Everybody knows what is going on in their own country so we used to share that kind of stuff as well. Sometimes we spent the whole night talking which is very interesting.

Thus it is interesting to note the variability in the negative and positive interpretations of international and home student relationships. This paradox in responses is also echoed in the study of home students' reactions to international students in the Harrison and Peacock study (2007). These interactions are highly complex and there are many factors that influence them, hence the complexity of the task (both for the student and for this book) of interpreting them.

Language issues in getting to know home students

Some of the international students and some of the UK home students in the Harrison and Peacock (2007) study considered that proficiency in language was an issue in the forming of relationships with home students. Pei believed that if her English were better she could make more friendships with other nationalities. She says:

> I think that if I spoke better English I could make more international friends.

Xan also feels that language is an obstacle to developing close relationships between himself and home students. He believes that this also explains his better relationships with other non-English international students. He considers that his international friends have similar levels of English and similar grasp of the language and thus are able to reach a better understanding of each other. He says:

> I think it's because of the language problem because if I speak English with the international students we are at the same level in the sense we can understand each other easily. And if I talk with the British I have the feeling that there is a like a barrier between us which is the language problem. I can't understand their accents perhaps and they can't understand mine. So I mean have some close British friends, like Donny who I used to fish with but [fewer] compared with my international student [friends].

On the other hand, it is interesting to note that Arin does not mention language as a barrier to more profound relationships. His English language skills are well developed and he has learned other languages (Norwegian, Danish and as a child Polish) to a high degree of competence. He does not quote his language as being a barrier to forming friendship, but rather he concentrates on issues of opportunity and social context. It may be that Arin's communicative competence, which he has developed in his time in other countries, is an advantage to him in overcoming any obstacles in communication with UK students.

So the role of language in relationships between international and home students seems to be a complex one. It appears that it is not only language that influences the development of relationships, but the complex interaction of other communicative factors such as communication skills, topics, goals and settings (Bonvillain, 2003). This again underscores the complexity of the relationships that this chapter is attempting to explore.

Age as a factor in international students' friendships

Another perceived obstacle to the success of relationships with home students is seen to be age and maturity. Arin states that he does not consider himself to be totally successful in his relationships in the UK because of his feeling that he cannot properly get to know home students. He believes that at least some of this is because of the age difference between himself and his classmates. He is 28 and a mature student and perceives himself to be more mature both in age and in terms of his outlook and personal preferences. He believes that this makes it difficult to succeed with a certain group of home students. When it is suggested to him that he is quite successful socially he says:

> Yeah but I would not say I was that successful...I went out with some UK students last week but there is still this age difference between us. They are interested in things that I am not. They do a lot more drinking and partying which I like to do but in a moderate fashion.
>
> Q. Are they younger than you?
>
> A. Yes, much younger. I am 28 and all those students are 18. I am a mature student, in the complete sense of this word.

It is interesting to note that Arin's relationship with the young students made him reflect upon himself and how he was when he was their age. He found their behaviour amusing sometimes (in a nice way) and in his reflection he had an opportunity to consider his own sense of himself and perceived himself as being more 'moderate' now that he is older. He said:

> I mean we're still really fine and joke together but you feel the difference, you feel more mature. Sometimes I can see myself when I was younger in the things that they're doing. I just laugh at them – in a positive way. It's just I just take it easier and they are just young kids who want to enjoy themselves. I have a different approach. I'm probably more moderate.

Although Arin talked about the fact that there was an age difference it is possible that it was not age but maturity that made the difference. Arin had a very close Indian friend who was much younger than him. His Indian friend Bridden was only 18, yet Arin felt that there was a close relationship between them and one that involved challenging intellectual exchange. Arin believed that his Chess Club friend Bribben was somehow 'older' than his 19 years. They often played chess together and 'challenged' each other in conversation too. Arin said:

> There is a young guy [Bribben] who is very smart and much more mature than his real age because he is just 18. So with him I'm more on the same level so we can talk about anything and he can challenge me and I can challenge him back. I mean he is still 18 but in many ways he is more aware of things such as politics and he is quite a religious guy. My conversation with him is more important and more serious.

Isken also echoes what Arin says about maturity being a factor in the lack of success of his relationships with UK students. He too appears to believe that the issue is not age but maturity and that this lack of maturity encourages Isken to gravitate towards the older UK students as they have a more serious approach to their studies. Isken says:

> I'm 20, most of them are my own age but I think I have more responsibility and maturity, whereas the younger students don't really take the work as seriously but a mature student does. In terms of getting on with the group work I used to get on really good with the mature students rather than the fresh undergraduates.

Isken mentions that the UK students go straight home after class and so again the opportunity to socialize is not there. But he also mentions the fact that when he was back at home he had the responsibility of looking after the house and his brothers and he considers that this may be a factor in the difference in maturity between himself and the home students. Isken's personal experience has been harder and he thus feels that he has developed more personal 'maturity', although maturity is a difficult attribute to define. Despite this, the issue of maturity could be seen as an influencing factor in the development of relationships between international and home students.

Relationships with home students: Worlds apart?

There was social contact between home and international students in this study, but home students seemed to remain on the periphery of the international networks. These friendships remained superficial and ephemeral. Generally the two groups had different 'stories', as Pei puts it, felt they have little in common, and were not part of each other's social groups. Arin thought that the home students did not go to lectures on a regular basis and he saw this as an obstacle to them getting to know each other better, as their contact remained, in his words, 'erratic'. This appears to be part of the geographical and physical distances that exist between international and home students. The focus of the students' lives is different and a form of campus versus town gap seems to have developed between them.

Shipton's (2005) study supports this finding, as in his study young undergraduate home students appeared to have a centre of gravity that was off campus whilst this study has shown that the focus of international students' university lives is on campus. Arin notes that his accommodation is too far away from the university, as he lives in a block of flats that is occupied by a majority of international students and is on the far side of the city centre, and he sees this as being an obstacle to getting to know home students better.

As well as geographical distance suggested through the data, there also seemed to emerge a temporal transience in the relationships built by the international network. Students were aware that the strong relationships they had developed were subject to the influence of time and space as at the end of their study they were likely to disappear. Arin talks about the transient nature of the university context and the fact that most students are going to leave the place where they are now and move somewhere else. This makes the relationships feel transient. He says he feels confident that if they did stay in touch they could become good friends as time passes and they have known each other longer.

Having said this, these aspects of university friendship and relationship do not appear so different from the relationships home students would have with each other. The Shipton study (2005) supports this, with the young UK undergraduates feeling that their time at university is transient and thus a 'time to really blow it', framed by an oppressive world of work. Although some students meet their friends for life when they go to university, many of the relationships developed by home students at university would be subject to the same impermanence as those of international students.

There is evidence here to suggest that shared interests can have an influence on the relationships of international and home students. Isken talks about his relationship with his tutor and says that the reason why they have become friendly is that they have a lot of interests in common. This is a recurring theme with other students in the study, as they see the development of friendship being based on shared interests. It is noticeable that there are fewer shared interests between international and home students. It may be that the difference in choice of activity in their social life drives an initial wedge between the two groups and underlines the geographical separation and the lack of opportunity to meet and develop relationships. Arin believes that there is no intrinsic reason why relationships between him and his home classmates cannot succeed. It is the mismatch in *modus vivendi* that limits the opportunities for relationships to develop further. This is supported in the findings of the Harrison and Peacock study (2007), showing that UK home students came to the conclusion that it was orientations to work rather than cultural backgrounds that influenced their choice of friendships.

So it is apparent from this discussion that there are strong, complex and varied influences on the relationships between international and home students. The more the international student network strengthens the less likely it may be that home students can become a part of this network. In addition to this, international students have more opportunity to meet other internationals and spend time together, as they are more likely to be together on campus, where they appear to spend most of their time. Home students are more likely to live in private accommodation in the city or with their family at home, often being engaged by part-time work that takes up a lot of their time and energy.

International students share common experiences, powerful experiences that relate to the fact that they have all moved from their home countries to a new cultural context. Because of this they are sharing a powerful learning experience that results from this transition, learning about 'otherness' and experiencing personal change as a result of this. International students share a strong common goal in the motivation to succeed and this, along with a well-defined view of the future, helps them to form a strong common bond. The strength of this bond is inclusive for those who share it but could also be exclusive to those who do not.

6 Preparing for Life in a Global Community?

This chapter considers how international students' experience of studying in Higher Education in another country may prepare them for living and working in a global context. It is noted in research on home students' experience (Ball et al., 2000; Shipton, 2005) that being at university changes students' perceptions of themselves and others. The nature of international students' experience may accentuate this development and provide them with a changed perspective on what it means to live, study and socialize with people from different cultures. This perspective could enable students to develop intercultural competences that may contribute to their professional and personal futures. This self-awareness and wider intercultural view of self being developed in the international student may be contrasted with a more monocultural experience of some home students who may not be benefiting from the social and cultural diversity being created by internationalization in Higher Education.

Caveat: A complex picture

The idea that international students form part of a global community is not intended to imply that this is a simple process involving uncomplicated transitions across communities. This chapter, and indeed this book as a whole, does not try to present what Holliday calls a 'neat global cosmopolitan dream' (2007a: 15). There is no suggestion here that international students study abroad in order to become internationalized from a 'western' viewpoint, that is, according to the 'west's' or the 'centre's' (Holliday, 2007a) definition of what it means to have an international outlook. There is no intention here to imply that the planet is a simple system of national societies extending to global villages (Bhabha, 1994).

Bhabha advocates a 'vernacular cosmopolitanism' that appreciates cultural experience from the 'minority' voice (ibid.), in this case the international student. It is the opportunity that Higher Education provides to meet and mix with other nationalities from across the globe that enables international students to develop an international perspective. However, the picture is complex and for this reason this book has presented a detailed picture of a particular context of Higher Education through the actual experiences and voices of international students. There is a need to understand cultural and cross-cultural experience as 'lived experience' (Holliday, 2007a) and it is essential that Higher Education can understand the 'lifeworld' of the student (Beard et al., 2007).

This chapter emphasizes the idea of participation in 'global communities' from a point of view of international students' perceptions of themselves as international. It is students' developing and changing sense of themselves as part of such a current and future international community that is important in this discussion, and there is no claim that a physical 'global community' exists independently of these perceptions.

The experience of spending time with students from other cultures, countries and communities may help students to develop an 'intercultural competence' (Byram, 1998) that could be advantageous to them in later life in both professional (Boud and Falchikov, 2006) and personal contexts.

Language, identity and change

The issue of language and identity is seminal to students' views of themselves as being 'international'. In particular, language development and competence is seen here as a factor that enables the development of an international or global perspective. Some definitions of language learning have seen language as 'social scaffolding for the development of the mind in interaction with others' (Kramsch, 2006: 98). This puts language and interaction at the centre of the development of our sense of ourselves and perceptions of others, and this is what enables us to construct the meanings that we call 'ourselves' (Kramsch, 2006: 99). There is also a crucial link between language and cultural identity and perceived personal attachment to present, past or imagined communities (ibid.). This supports the idea that international students' development of language and interaction with others may influence their perception of themselves as part of a 'global community'.

Language and communication are much more than simple means of passing information from person to person. Language is strongly bound up with our social identities and our use of language aligns us with social groups and cultural practices (Byram and Fleming, 1998). When people move from one social context to another and meet with speakers of other languages there is a sense in which negotiation of meanings in language is necessary. For communication to be successful it is essential that speakers across cultures have the same understandings of the deeper, culturally specific, pragmatic meanings of language. Thus, as international students move from one cultural and social environment to another and there are a number of linguistic environments surrounding their new context, there may be a process of reconstruction of meaning through their new social network. In a sense this occurs in order that a new social 'reality' may be constructed. Byram and Fleming describe a similar process occurring through language learning:

> Only after a process of discovering those meanings and practices [in the new environment] can learners negotiate and create a new reality with their interlocutors, one which is new to both learners and interlocutors, a shared world of interactions and experience. (1998: 2–3)

This new social reality is what Bhabha termed the 'third space', a third and new 'culture' that is formed by the meeting and mingling of two different cultures (1994). The concept of the 'third space' is an interesting one in terms of this discussion, as it is a means of explaining the process at work when individuals from a particular context move to a new cultural and linguistic context and, through interaction with others, a third culture or space develops.

The 'third space' is a highly complex concept, but is useful here as it moves away from the idea of culture being a fixed or immovable feature. Bhabha's idea of a shifting and changing hybrid culture negates the idea of cultural essentialism where preset ideas of culture and nationality breed stereotype (Holliday, 2004). 'Third space' is a construct that seeks to explain the personal and cultural development of an individual and assumes that 'cultures are dynamic systems which are constantly renegotiated and cultural meaning is created through the interactions of speakers/writers' (Finkbeiner, 2005). This emphasis on the individual puts personal identity at the centre of culture and, in terms of the educational process, suggests that learners' prior knowledge, beliefs and values are central to the process of attaining intercultural competence (Byram, 1998).

Considering the issue of identity from the point of view of the international student, it is interesting to note that upon coming to a new educational context international students are continually forced to restate and renegotiate their identity. The question 'where are you from?' is probably the one that international students are asked the most frequently, and this requires them to reassociate themselves with their national origin. In one sense this constant reaffirming of the link between their nationality and their identity is a force that emphasizes national stereotypes both in the eyes of the person asking the question and, perhaps reluctantly, in the eyes of the international student (Bochner et al., 1977). Thus it may be that when the actual boundaries of culture are more strongly emphasized it may be more difficult for these to be crossed. It is perhaps in concentrating on the national boundaries and the lines that divide groups of students that isolation is continued.

Although international students are seemingly encouraged to identify and define themselves according to their nationalities, there is a strong sense in which their experience of moving to a new social and cultural context enables them to achieve a development in their perception of themselves and others. One does not have to go abroad to achieve this development, as education itself can be a catalyst for this. However, the intensity of the experience of travelling abroad can perhaps initiate or accentuate this type of development. Iredale (1994) notes the power of the experience of living in a different country and its value in shaping the future of an intercultural person. He states:

> Even to move to another culture is to be touched by major influences, as those of us who have lived in other countries and cultures know. The enormous changes of perception that new cultural and educational experiences can work are an important influence in the formation of people's working lives as well as on their personal development. (Iredale, 1994: 7)

The process of these changes in perception may take place through a form of 'reflexivity', a process through which learners first consider themselves and their own 'culture', then can see the culture and social identities of others in a new and interesting light.

Language as a means of gaining entry to a global community

The students in the study saw language as a means of learning to live with others and learn about the culture of the new context. It appears that English was viewed as an international language that may allow students to gain entry into a more global arena.

Improving English language skills was seen by students to be very important. They tended to view this as part of the purpose of their time at university, and not simply as a tool to support their studies but as an achievement in its own right. Many aspects of their reasons for wanting to improve their language related to their desire to live, work and be with others in an international context. English Language skills were viewed by students as an important qualification that might enable them to access a global community.

To this end, students appeared to be often searching for ways of improving their English. Their desire for relationships with home students seems to be part of this aim. If they have friendships with English-speaking students this is a way of improving their language skills. Arin supports this suggestion when he says that he believes the only effective way to learn a language is to live in that country and mix with its people. He berates the approach to language teaching in his home country and suggests that learning a language must be experiential. He says:

> From my experience, to learn a foreign language you actually have to live in that foreign country [and] interact with people. I was studying English in Italy but I have to say that the way they teach it is appalling. They concentrate very much on the grammar. Most of my skills in English and other languages, I learn them [in] the field.

The need to mix with English speakers as a way of gaining exposure to English is also important to Pei. She reports that she and her closest Chinese friends have tried to speak English to each other in order to improve their language, but this is very difficult to sustain. She says:

> Sometimes we try to speak English. We cannot speak English the whole day, just one or two hours. Even that's better than nothing. Yes it's better. We try to speak English.

So it is difficult to talk in English when you know both interlocutors could communicate more effectively in their own language. However, if one is determined to do so this is still possible. Pei talks about an experience when she met someone and began speaking English but then was surprised to discover that her new friend was also Chinese. Following this discovery, they both continued to speak to each other in English. Pei says:

> I sat with a young lady she told me she was from the MBA course and so we talked with each other and at first we didn't know each other so we spoke English. But later [laughs] we realised we were both from China and I said we would speak Chinese but we still spoke English. I was very surprised. Yeah, I thought she would speak Chinese but she always spoke English to me [so] I thought I better speak English to her [laughs]. We just spoke English all the time, very interesting.

This contradicts the commonly cited stereotype of international students choosing to speak in their own language. Pei desires to speak in English as much as possible, and, in the face of lack of opportunities with British speakers, speaks English to other Chinese people. It also raises interesting issues relating to language as a means of expressing one's identity (Sysoyev, 2002). In the interaction above Pei got to know someone through her second language before they realized that they shared a first language. To Pei this seemed an unusual way of getting to know someone and she found it an interesting and new experience.

Our impressions of our 'selves'

There was a strong sense that the students reflected upon themselves and their experiences both before they came to university abroad and after their arrival. The idea that they felt themselves to be 'open' and 'sociable' was one that recurred frequently. Students linked this both with their description of their friendship group and with their perceived success in developing their social networks. Arin says about himself:

> Well I find it quite, quite easy to mingle with people and ... I don't find it very difficult to get along with people ... and for some reason I find it easier to mingle with people who come from other countries because maybe it's the fact that we have something in common, the fact that we're coming from a different background and joining a new culture ...

This echoes Sera's desire to mix internationally, but Arin takes it further by indicating that his successful friendship group is a result of this personal ability to 'get along with others'. In a similar way, Xan also sees part of himself as a person being that he likes to meet new people and talk to them. He also sees this as an aspect of his success socially. He says:

> Like, that's part of my personality I like to make friends with everybody. I know a lot of people from different backgrounds. Since I [came here from] Indonesia I can talk differently. For example I can talk with my high-class friends or anyone. And I can have a nice informal chat with for example cleaners from my area. You know I like to talk to everyone.

Xan believes his interactions with others are different since he came to the UK. He has developed an ability to adapt and to be able to talk to different types of people. This could be seen as an important skill for life beyond university.

Identity and development of 'self'

There is a sense in which international students have come to study abroad to achieve an independence of self. Students' descriptions of their personal motivations for being mobile indicate that it is almost a 'rite of passage' which will enable them to find themselves and establish themselves as individuals. Arin talks about the difference in levels of independence for him when he is abroad. He says he feels he is an independent sort of person but needed to come here partly to get his independence from his family. He says:

> In Italy because it's not easy to actually part from your parents because it is not very easy to find a good job and so I guess I had to go abroad also to achieve my independence.

In addition to independence of self, there is also an interesting issue of students' talk about their developing perseverance. Many of the students talk about trying hard and continuing to struggle until they succeed socially or academically. This is a commonly recurring theme and may suggest that they feel that their perseverance in their experience here is a particular aspect of how they have developed personally. In addition to this, their sense of their own ability to persevere suggests a growth in esteem and indicates that students may feel they have succeeded. This development of self through the experience of being abroad is an interesting facet of students' personal growth through their education.

There is an interesting issue around the idea of adaptability and changing nature of self. Isken talks about retaining a professional relationship within the university and how he changes his approach to fit his different situations. Xan also talks at length about his sense of himself being adaptable and having an ability to change according to context and to whom he is speaking. Isken sees himself as easy-going and relaxed (like Arin) and says himself that he can adapt to a changing environment. This seems to be another strong commonality that some students have seen as key to their social and academic success.

The students in the study that supports this book seem to be people who are skilled in changing and shifting roles according to context. The students' sense of themselves as being flexible and changeable perhaps also underlines their need for reference points both within their friendship groups (the anchor of their own nationality described above) and in retaining their relationships with their family. It may be that their experience as international students here has enabled them to be more adaptable and open to change in both context and relationships.

Development of a global community

This section of the chapter considers the idea that the international student could be part of the development of a global community. The nature of their sustained relationships with friends and family back home is an example of how their network stretches out and crosses cultural and national boundaries. The students appeared to use modern technology as a means of maintaining and developing their international network both within the UK and beyond.

Getting support from friends and family back home

There remained a very strong link between the students and family back home, despite the geographical distance. Contact with parents and family was very frequent. A number of students reported daily contact with family. This contact was interpreted by the students as being very important to their emotional welfare and a basic motivator in their drive to carry on with their studies. One of the students from the Chess Club believes that his contact with his father helps him to continue and also keeps him in touch with his 'previous identity'. It is almost as though he needs to remember who he was before he came to university and reassure himself that his previous life is 'still there'. He says:

> Some people will find this strange but I email my dad every day. We keep in touch every day. With my family it's very important but with my friends from school it's occasional. I think it's very important because it does give you a sense of constructiveness. If you think that you've truly lost all contact from home and then you might think where am I and where are my friends. But if you're in touch with your family you know that they will always be there. I think that they keep you going.

Although this student thinks he is unusual in this, in fact other students also report this daily contact. When asked if she gets support from family back home, Pei says:

> [I keep in touch with] my parents, my brothers and sisters in China because we can email each other every day. Also phone them. Sometimes I was in a bad mood and I wrote to my parents and they wrote back to encourage me.

There is a strong sense that this contact with those at home also provides moral, psychological and emotional support that in turn helps students to continue. Isken underlines the importance to him of this contact. He says:

> I love keeping in touch with them. I write an email every day to my friends. Friends back home are very important, they give moral support. They say just go ahead, don't worry all of your projects will go well. What are you up to these days, how are you, how are your studies? Why don't you try and don't be afraid.

Students also interpret this contact as directly supporting them in their study by providing immediate motivation. Xan explains how he feels when he has spoken to his family. He says:

> It makes me like more energetic, you know sometimes I just have one chapter left or a conclusion and the fact that they ask makes me like see it's important to get finished quickly. They motivate me, yeah.

He underlines this by saying:

> Sometimes your spirit just fails and you lose your ability to study. Then close contact with your family is really important.

Even in the case of Arin, who is a more mature student of 28 years of age, his relationship with his family and friends is important as a point of reference in times of difficulty. It also keeps him up to date with what is happening back home, but the most important aspect of his relationship with those back home is with his parents. He says:

> I like to hear everything is fine back home and my parents are all right and hear what they are planning to do. It's quite important, well you know it's kind of moral support and something you will always refer to if you are in trouble. Also I like to hear from my friends what's going on at home, what's happening with their lives. It's quite important, especially the relationship with my parents. It's quite important.

So the international students perceive there to be a direct link between academic motivation and their contact with those back home. There are potential explanations for this, such as the fact that their parents are funding them or that the geographical distance makes the wishes of those back home appear more significant. However, it seems that for these international students the strength and importance of home ties are magnified by their experience abroad, and these relationships play an important part in the friendships they are developing here and influence their social and learning experience.

As may be expected, however, there is variation in these relationships with parents and it appears that Marcus' contact with his parents is less frequent and possibly less significant to him. He says that he has travelled a lot in the last three years and this has decreased the strength of his contact with those back home. He is still in regular contact with his parents, but this becomes less frequent as the year goes on and as he reassures them that he is doing well.

Arin also notes that he still retains a measure of self-reliance in terms of his contact with those back home. He suggests that he would not necessarily worry his parents by contacting them if he were homesick. He indicates that this is an aspect of his own personality and he would tend to work out these difficulties for himself. The following is a touching and detailed picture of Arin's relationship with his parents. He says:

> I like talking to my father and hearing that everything is alright, and hearing from my mother, just making sure they are doing okay ... I try not to worry them, life goes on. I don't call them crying that I want to go back home ... because I was too proud – I didn't ever call them and say I want to come back home. It's just me. I just don't do those things.

The significance of the relationship between these international students and their parents perhaps shows that the support that they lack in geographically immediate contexts is replaced by contacts that are retained with those at home. This support also appears to provide a sense of continuity in the students' sense of their relationships with others. Students feel that the presence of these relationships in their new context abroad makes sense and gives a feeling of security. It also identifies students as belonging to a wider community, one that stretches across national borders and over geographical distance.

The future

The international students appeared to have quite set and well-formulated views of what the future holds for them. Their travelling abroad to study was part of their plan for the future and their hope is that this will be a gateway for them to a better and more successful global future.

Chiang describes his plans, and it is clear that he has thought about them at length and has a determination to see them carried out. He wants to get a good grade in his degree and then has plans to work abroad in Europe, America or Australia. However, he does not want to stay abroad forever, but has definite plans to return to Shanghai as that is his home and he thinks it is a very good place to live. He says:

> First I want to study a Master's Degree. After that I want to see if I've got some chance to work here or in the United States or Australia or the European Union. I may stay for that but if not I will go to Shanghai. Finally I must go back because it's my home, it's my home city and I like that city; actually it's a really good city.

Chiang would like to spend time in Europe or America and this is part of his plans for the future. These experiences working outside China will be an asset for him when he returns and may enable him to get a better job. He is reflecting upon his future, and all of the ideas for what he wants are related to achieving the same goal; a good job and an international lifestyle where he can travel freely abroad. He says:

> But for me you know I do really wish to get some work experience overseas. It can help me to find a good job in Shanghai and if I stay in other countries more than three or five years I may become the permanent resident of that country. As a Chinese it's very difficult for us to get a visa to travel around the world. I really want to get some passport or residence from a developed country. But my final destination is Shanghai.

Chiang has a clear picture of the next years of his life and is sure and determined that he will return to his home with positive advantage from his time abroad.

Arin also has very well-formulated views of what his future holds. He has had these views from the time he first left Italy, and even on his first stay abroad in Iceland he felt he was to travel further, despite the fact that he could have settled down in Scandinavia. He was driven by his own perception of what the future should be for him. He says:

> I could probably settle down somewhere in this country. I can speak Danish and Norwegian so I could have settled down there as well but I always wanted to get a degree, and get a nice job, a skilled job. I could have settled down and worked as a social worker in Iceland but I wanted also to do something more, to get a degree and do something more challenging intellectually. So I went for it.

His vision of the future is, like Chiang's, an international one where he is freer to travel and to work abroad than he was before. Like Chiang, he hopes that his degree is a passport to being 'international' and enables him to have more options in the future. He says:

> So that's the main reason I decided to come here to the UK; good English and a British degree is of more value internationally. Perhaps in the future if I wanted to work somewhere else like Australia, a UK degree has this extra value.

These well-formed visions of the future are in contrast to the home students in the Shipton (2005) study. In this study the young undergraduate home students did not have a strong vision of what they would do next when their degree finished, and in some ways the degree was not part of their view of what the future would hold for them.

Finally, the international students' vision of their future does not involve the people they spend time with and depend on now. Despite the fact that they are very close to their international student group, they appear to be conscious that they do not have shared futures. They would remain friends and close if they were to stay in the same place, but, sadly, once away from this context they will probably lose contact. Arin says:

> It all depends you know where we end up. Many students are probably going to move somewhere else. I mean I'm pretty sure that if we stay in contact we could be good friends. They'll probably mature and have families.

This awareness of the fact that their futures may not be shared is perhaps something that emphasizes the functional and purposeful nature of their friendships. So, despite the closeness of some of the relationships formed on campus and in the new context, there is also the sense that these bonds are transient. Close friends finish their courses and leave to return home or go on to get work elsewhere.

Even when relationships are of the same nationality there is a sense that these associations may not last. Xan's girlfriend is also from Indonesia, and he sees her as one of his closest relationships, but they are not sure what will happen and whether they will continue to see each other when they return to Indonesia. The conversation with Xan is as follows:

> Q. Your girlfriend's Indonesian, isn't she, do you think you might keep in touch with her when you go back home?
>
> A. I don't know, she's still got three years to be here and she's still young and I've got to go back to my career back home so we don't know yet.

Many of these aspects of friendship and relationship do not appear so different from the relationships home students would have with each other, and the transience of university relationships may also be evident for these students. On the other hand, many home students meet their friends for life when they go to university and keep in touch well into later life. In the case of international students, geographical distances make future contact more unsure. The international student group has a strong bond, but it is dependent on the context and serves a purpose at a particular time in these students' lives.

Citizens of the international community?

So the international students in this study seemed to have very clear views of how their futures would develop after they had finished their course. They saw themselves as future citizens of the international or global community, and this was also bound up with their belief that their futures would be a success because of their experiences here.

There is a sense in which students in this study considered themselves to be preparing to become citizens of an international or global community. Chiang talks about his study in the UK becoming a 'passport' for him to travel, and, despite the fact that he wants to return to his home city of Shanghai, he feels that he would like to spend time in other countries. There is a sense in which this has become part of Chiang's education, and the process of achieving his educational goals incorporates a process of personal internationalization.

Since the idea of the global village has come into common usage, the suggestion that people across the globe have somehow become more 'connected' has gathered pace within the educational setting. This may, of course, be an idealized perception of international relationships, and it is useful to note Holliday's caveat against constructing a neat and idealized global community (Holliday, 2007a). However, computers and the internet have given immediacy to communication across distance. Through the medium of information technologies and through education students are learning to think of themselves as global citizens, seeing the world, and their place in the world, in ways very different from their parents. Today's global networks create connections between people which span time and distance in ways the world has never before seen, and with implications which are beginning to have major political, social, and educational implications (Toffler, 1990).

7 Concluding Comments to the Research

This chapter draws together some of the main issues that have been raised throughout this book. In particular it presents a summary of some of the themes of the research project that underpins this book.

The themes of the research

A strong international community

One of the students, Bridden, who was a student from the Chess Club, was reflecting on the importance of his frequent contact with his family back home and he suggested that these geographically distant relationships helped him to carry on because they gave meaning to the new relationships he was making. He said this measure by which he could judge his current relationships was very important because 'otherwise life is just a series of lost relationships'.

The strong international network seems to prevent the students from feeling that their social relationships are transient because they have moved away to study abroad. The students arrived in a new environment where they were initially alone. They appeared to spend a difficult first stage feeling lonely and lost, but by the time they had reached their second or third year at university they had emerged from this difficult phase. They had made the effort to build a social group that replaced the one in their home environment, yet close links with the network back home were retained and even became heightened in their significance. The students' social experience perhaps also highlights the value and importance of their ties with family and their sense of their own identity. As a way of avoiding 'losing' relationships past and present, the network becomes of paramount importance.

This international network can be said to partly represent the outcome of a university drive to internationalize. The human product of this global force is a diverse international group who come together for a short period of time but learn from each other and view their relationships and mutual support as part of their overall learning experience.

As their relationships develop over their time here, they form a definite view of their futures as being international and global in nature. Their experience abroad amongst their international friends prepares them to live and work in a community that has a global perspective.

Developing independence

An interesting contrast to the strength of the international student social network and its possible development as a community of practice is the sense that these international students are also fiercely independent. This is interesting, because the strength of the group feeling amongst the students would suggest that they need the group to survive and could not succeed without its support. On the contrary, two students note that, although their social group is very important to them, they also perceive it to be replaceable. Pei says that to some extent she depends on her friends but that if she did not have her friends she would still carry on and would make other friends in their place. Sera notes that she feels she needs her friends, but without them she would still carry on, although her experience here would be of an inferior quality.

It appears that the international students' period of isolation when they first arrived may have equipped them with the skills to continue with limited social support. In addition to this, the support of the relationships they have at a distance enables them to be confident that there remains some stability in their social relationships.

The deficit model?

Some of the discussion in this book has mentioned a deficit model of viewing international students. It may be that this relates to expectations that are formulated before the student arrives at university abroad. As far as 'getting to know British culture' and relationships with home students are concerned, there are expectations before international students arrive that this will be a part of their educational experience. The UKCOSA study (Merrick, 2004) supports this suggestion and indicates that getting to know British students is one of the biggest concerns that international students have before they arrive in the UK. Despite this, it appears that, whilst international students do develop relationships with home students, these relationships remain superficial and are on the periphery of the international student's network.

However, it appears from the students in this group that by the time they have been at university for a year or more they have moved beyond perceiving this as a deficit and they express positive views about their international network. The students in the research that supports this book seem to appreciate their strong and supportive international network, and the peripheral nature of their relationships with home students no longer appears to them to be an issue. It seems that assumptions that it is a necessity for international students to form bonds with home students should be questioned. It may be that international students value the international group they have constructed and may not be missing anything by their lack of profound contact with home students. On the other hand, it is entirely possible that home students could gain a more global perspective through more contact with international students.

Language issues

The issue of language and its influence on the international student experience is significant. Pei, Xan and Chiang all note that language is an issue which affects in forming closer relationships with home students. Difficulties with pronunciation or regional accent and vocabulary are cited as issues in this respect. However, interestingly, language is not cited as an issue in forming relationships with other international students, despite the fact that the international student network described here has a large number of different language speakers. It may be that international students have a similar or equal level of language competence and sociocultural competence in English and thus they develop strategies to enable them to understand each other more effectively. It seems that, whilst language is an important issue in the development of strong bonds, language is possibly being used as an explanatory concept alongside culture to apportion responsibility for the superficiality of the relationships between home and international students.

As a case in point, Arin does not cite language as being an issue for him in terms of his relationships with home students. He sees the issue as being one of opportunity rather than language, with limited chances to meet due to the two groups having a different 'centre of gravity' (Shipton, 2005) in their social lives. It is interesting to consider whether Arin's perception of language not being an obstacle to developing relationships with home students is related to the fact that he has travelled quite widely and has had experience of communicating with speakers of other languages, having lived for an extended period in Iceland before his arrival at university. This may give him a communicative competence beyond that of students who had not lived in another country previous to their stay at university abroad. This raises the question of the relationship between language competence (in a second language) and tolerance and understanding of others' differences. In learning another language we also learn about another culture, and as a result of this we may learn empathy and tolerance of other peoples and their differences.

Age and maturity

The issue of international students' perception of themselves as being more mature than their home student classmates emerged as important. Many of the students talk about this maturity difference despite the fact that age differences may not be that great in actual years. Arin is 28 years old and feels that he is very much more mature than his home student counterparts, who are in their early 20s. He says: 'I am a mature student in the complete sense of this word.' Arin feels he has more maturity or experience of the world. In fact it appears that the difference is in outlook rather than years, and this may be as a result of the differences in experience from before students come abroad to university. This is strongly underlined by the description of early and previous personal and educational experiences provided by Isken in the postscript to this book.

Xan very much sees the construction of the cultural East–West split as a split in generations rather than between his culture and UK culture. He sees a great difference between himself and some people of his own nationality, and emphasizes that this is an age issue. It appears that he has already reflected extensively on this issue and sees himself as modern and young, in contrast to the older generation, whom he perceives to be traditional and reactionary. Many of these views might also be bound up with religion, and Xan is a Catholic brought up in a predominantly Muslim country, which may perhaps for him underline differentiation between groups such as old and young, traditional and modern.

On another note relating to age and relationships, there are older groups of people who are making contact with international students in the UK. This often occurs through church groups or where people have spent time abroad in their youth and have an idea that they would like to return the hospitality they experienced in another country. Students are often invited for festivals such as Christmas or Easter, or sometimes just for Sunday lunch. This may lead international students to draw conclusions about the younger generation being less generous with their time, whereas their views of the older generation in the UK are that they are kind and have time to talk and help them. Isken, Pei and Xan have experience of these kinds of links with a community outside the university. The friendliness and support of these relationships appear in contrast to the more distant relationships the international student group have experienced with the younger home students at the university.

Prejudice and preconceived ideas

Some preconceptions about home students, and in particular their attitude to learning, appeared to be a barrier to the development of more positive academic and social exchange between international and home students. There is a recurring sense that there are some prejudgements on the part of the international students which affect their openness to home students with whom they come into contact.

The stereotype of the British as being 'reserved' is quoted by Arin as being the reason that it is difficult to get to know home students. Expanding on this, he feels that if another person makes the first move towards being friendly with home students then there is the potential to get to know them better. There appears to Arin to be a lack of effort on their part and a sense that home students are holding back until someone else makes that effort. One source of these preconceptions could stem from the limited experience students have in mixing with their home student counterparts, particularly in class. Preconceptions which already exist can be emphasized by a lack of contact and thus a pattern of relationships is established.

The international students seem to perceive home students to lack motivation and to be predominantly interested in having a good time and drinking. They say that it is difficult to make strong academic relationships with them because they do not attend class regularly enough. Perhaps it is because this drinking culture is so well advertized on campus that international students might make assumptions about the motivation of all home students. This is an issue that could influence continuing stereotypes of both home and international students. These preconceptions extend also into the classroom, where students quite frequently remain in their separate nationality groups and make assumptions about each other from physical behaviour such as where people sit.

Having said this, the research also showed that there were some positive and constructive relationships between international students and home students. There are reports of useful and positive relationships built around the academic context. Arin, Isken, Chiang and Xan all said that they had good relationships with coursemates and that they had experienced academic exchange in group work that has engendered mutual respect. Chiang talks of social relationships that have come from interaction with home students, and Isken had worked very positively with the mature female home students on his course.

So it is interesting to note the variability in the negative and positive interpretations of international and home student relationships. This paradox in responses is also echoed in the study of UK home students' reactions to international students in the Harrison and Peacock study (2007) mentioned earlier in this book. The social interaction that takes place in the complex social environment of the university in the 21st century is fraught with tensions that relate to culture, social status, educational background and differences in views on the role of education in society.

Summary

The central chapters of this book have attempted to present a detailed picture of the international student experience in Higher Education. From this detailed view of international students in their educational context the book has considered some of the issues relating to their experience, including those of friendship, language, culture and identity, and how they might affect students' view of their educational context.

The preceding chapters have shown that the influences on the international student experience are many and complex. The institutional and national drives towards internationalization have a contextual influence. Social networks and groups that form communities of practice can become part of international students' social capital. Culture, language and their influence on students' sense of self are all seen as crucial to a contextualized understanding of the lived experience of the international student in Higher Education.

The students' experiences presented here have suggested that the social context of learning can be a means of building social capital that can improve the quality of learning experiences. The international students talked about actively constructing their social context, and, through the development of a community of practice, a positive and purposeful learning community emerged. The community of practice developed through the students' shared learning experience could exert an influence on the way that students perceive themselves as part of the student community and indeed the wider global community beyond the university.

Learning experiences in a new social and academic environment may be a force for a change in perception. Students may develop skills and competences as a result of their experiences that could help them to work and live in a global community. This community might consist of the travelled and those who have learned about themselves as an 'intercultural person'.

Part 3
Discussion

8 Paths towards an International Experience for All: the Criticality of Discourse, Context and Internationalization at Home

This chapter focuses on a selection of issues that are drawn from previous discussions in the book. The examination of these issues aims to move towards an alternative perspective on the international experience, developing a way of focusing not exclusively on the international student group but on the learning community as a whole. As a first step towards this alternative framework, the chapter will consider the power of the discourse with which we frame the international experience. From there, alternative ways of thinking about teaching and learning in an international context will be suggested and the importance of the context of learning will be discussed. Finally the idea of internationalization at home will be examined as an alternative way to view international education, and some example cases of this approach will be presented.

The influence of discourse

The words and narratives chosen to define aspects of our lives are part of a discourse that also circulates an ideology in a particular cultural context. These ideologies carry values relating to how we understand particular concepts and are often used to privilege the position of particular groups and 'naturalize' the inferiority of other groups (Shirato and Yell, 2000). There are discourses around internationalization in

Higher Education that may be influencing the student experience and the way that we view the role of international students in our universities. For example, it has been suggested here that the term 'culture' may be a misleading one, a 'blame concept' that can be used to explain away difficulties in interaction that may have occurred (Spencer-Oatey, 2000). These discourses were discussed in Chapter 1 and were also considered in the discussion of the data that has been presented in this book. These current ways of speaking about international education often revolve around binaries such as 'Eastern' and 'Western' scholarship; 'international' and 'home' students; 'collectivist' and 'individualist' cultures; deep and surface learning; all of which simply serve to polarize communities in Higher Education. These binaries are what Ryan and Louie (2007) term the 'false dichotomy' of our dealings with internationalization. The broad brush strokes of the labels applied to students 'home' and 'international' refer to ideals and models that do not bear much resemblance to the 'real' people who study in universities. Debates on educational terms such as 'criticality' in Higher Education are seldom based on a clear understanding of what the terms denote and often suggest that 'Western' systems are superior, ignoring the complexities and diversity inherent in different education systems (ibid.).

The research detailed in this book has indicated that both international and home students have preconceived ideas about the social and academic motivations of the other group. Their generalized, crude understandings of each other are often manifested in the ways they describe each other and the way cultural groups are constructed. A recent study supports the suggestion that there is a discourse and an attending ideology that characterize the interaction between 'home' and international students. Peacock and Harrison's (2009) study of the attitudes of UK students towards international students found that the students often used wide geographic terms to describe international students by continent (e.g. Africa or Asia), by broad ethnicities (e.g. Chinese, Indian) or by religion (mainly 'Muslim' in this category) (Peacock and Harrison, 2009). However, Peacock and Harrison also found that the groups of international students who were from European, Anglophone and Latin American backgrounds were characterized in a much more specific way, described as being 'just like us', and the UK students made a point of noting personal details such as names and exact countries of origin.

The use of names as opposed to ethnic labels suggests an accommodation towards particular groups of students who are considered 'near' in cultural terms. The reasons behind this feeling of similarity would benefit from further research. However, referring back to Lee and Rice's study (2007) discussed in Chapter 2, which found that students of 'white' racial origin perceived there to be less prejudice against them, there may be a racial issue in students' perceptions of who is 'in' their group. The issue of discourse is of crucial importance here, as the prejudice noted above is inherent in the words students use to describe each other. Previous studies, including this one, have indicated that these perceptions of each other and the 'other' can be dispelled by active experience of working together (Volet and Ang, 1998) and coming to know individuals as real people.

Whilst it is unrealistic to suggest that we cease to use terms such as 'international', geographic or ethnic labels such as the ones discussed above or problematic conceptual terms such as 'culture', these terms and concepts need to be used with an awareness of their complexity. A more considered approach to the language we use to describe each other and the learning context in which we interact in Higher Education may go some way to improving intercultural interaction. We should also consider ways forward in our approaches to internationalization that will take account of situatedness of social, educational and cultural practices in universities (Ryan and Louie, 2007).

Ways of thinking about teaching and learning practices in an international context

This section suggests ways of thinking about teaching and learning in an international context. Some current perceptions of international education still imply that 'Western' education is intrinsically superior. Haigh (2008) notes that the cultural hybridity that is allowed in contemporary Higher Education has limits and it is still the case that 'Western' educational norms prevail. In other words, there remains an implicit agreement, often inherent in discourses used, that international education is a one-way street and 'they should learn from us' (Haigh, 2008: 430). The following paragraphs of this section suggest some ways of thinking about international education that may encourage diverse perspectives on learning.

Teaching and learning are culturally embedded

It is important to recognize that approaches to teaching, learning and assessment are in themselves culturally embedded. Trahar (2008) notes that the 'Western' academy can be seen as a 'colonising institution' through its 'subtle treatment of those who do not belong to its dominant culture' (2008: 3). This dominant culture is implicit in our teaching methods, which may, albeit inadvertently, imply that students need to free themselves from their previous learning identities in order to be successful in a 'Western' educational system.

The discourses we use in Higher Education should not suggest that students need to conform to the practices of the dominant culture. Examples of approaches to internationalization provided later in this chapter suggest that some interactive pedagogies may provide a space for both students and staff to include critical reflections on their own and others' backgrounds. This collaborative approach may make it clear to students that their sociocultural contexts may be relevant and indeed crucial to the curriculum they are studying. Trahar suggests that we should not just see diversity as a positive aspect of education, but that we should move towards exploring diversity as part of the 'lived experience' of teaching and learning in a particular context (2008: 11). This is very much the philosophy that this book has tried to expound in its presentation of the lived experience of a group of international students.

This way of seeing teaching and learning as part of a wider experience may require us to rethink the narrower conceptions of learning that rely on assumptions of previous experience. For example, it may be useful to abandon our adherence to the idea of particular 'learning styles' as being associated with particular groups of international students (as discussed in Chapter 2). Instead, it may be more effective to consider the wide variety of Higher Educational contexts as diverse 'learning cultures' that are highly complex environments. A learning culture could be viewed as a complex environment made up of the interplay of teachers, learning tasks, students and their backgrounds, and, rather than emphasizing courses or programmes, this approach would foreground the significance of the interactions and practices that take place within this culture (Davies and Ecclestone, 2008).

Seeing similarity instead of difference

As part of the process of acknowledging the complexity of learning cultures, it is useful to focus on the similarities between social, cultural and educational backgrounds. The majority of the research that has been carried out in relation to the role of international students in Higher Education focuses on how they are different in their backgrounds to learning. Little research has considered how similar our personal experience of education may be.

Teekens notes that global developments in economy and information technology are 'resulting in patterns of living that are becoming increasingly similar in all countries and for all peoples' (2000: 29). Many of the issues facing the international student group are those that face all students, and indeed all of us as people. The conversations detailed in this book and the extensive amounts of time spent in observation with students provided an insight into some quite emotional moments of students' lives. There were some moving descriptions of conversations with family back home, for example. These are descriptions of human experiences rather than being specific to the culture of a group and they show something which is true about everyone. We all miss family and friends when we are far away from them. This emphasizes that there are many elements of international communities that underline how similar we are to each other, rather than how different.

Further to this, Harrison (2007) notes that there is a dearth of research that addresses the issue of diversity within the international student population. This book has aimed to address this by showing diversity among international students and presenting a detailed picture of international students as real people with faults and prejudices, such as Chiang's conscious decision to associate only with certain groups of students.

The relationship between informal and formal learning

The research presented in this book has underlined the importance of the social context of learning. The student experience examined here suggests that there is a link between this social or informal learning and the more formal learning associated with the curriculum and classroom. Much of what has been written about informal learning has focused on 'work-place' learning, but relatively little research has acknowledged the importance of social learning beyond the classroom, although there is a recent increased focus on the physical social spaces where learning takes place. There are also other initiatives that are aiming to informalize learning, such as the moves towards mentoring schemes in Higher Education and increased use of classroom assistance and 'buddies' in schools (Hodkinson, Colley and Malcolm, 2003). It is important to acknowledge that learning does take place through everyday embodied practices and in non-educational settings (ibid.). In the case of mobile students who are studying and working in a new cultural context, this informal learning is magnified and is focused on learning about diversities and similarities in people and practices.

This book has focused on friendships and understanding the role of friendships in informal learning contexts. The relationships and strong social networks appeared to provide added value to the learning of the formal classroom, and may have played a part in enabling students to continue and to succeed in their studies at university. Further research into the role of informal learning (and its relationship with achievement) may also enable us to understand why some students succeed whilst others drop out.

It appears that one of the keys to improving intercultural interaction and international experiences in Higher Education is the link between informal and formal curricula, and this is underlined by recent work on the necessity of acknowledging learning beyond the formal curriculum (Clifford, 2009). Leask (2009) notes that improved interactions between home and international students are dependent on the way we use both the formal and the informal curricula to encourage and reward intercultural engagement. Earlier sections of this book have argued that intercultural interaction is a key outcome of an internationalized curriculum, and Leask argues (ibid.) that this requires a campus environment and culture that motivate and reward interaction between international and home students both inside and outside the classroom.

The importance of context

This book has strongly emphasized the role and relevance of social, cultural and academic context in the learning experience. Early research relating to the friendship patterns and social relationships of international students (Bochner et al., 1977; Lee and Rice, 2007) examined in Chapter 2 indicated that social context can exert an influence on students' views of each other. An underlying premise of this book has been to establish that these social relationships can enhance the student learning experience, and therefore a question should be asked about the factors in the learning environment that can promote more positive and effective academic and social relationships between student groups.

Recent research carried out by the author has suggested that particular types of learning environment can produce positive responses to intercultural interaction. The study, which considered how student views of collaborative group work in a diverse international academic context may have changed in the last decade, set up a retrospective review of a research project carried out in 1998 that investigated students' views of working in international groups (Montgomery, 2009). The research of Volet and Ang (1998) in Australia considered factors that students believed to be affecting the formation of mixed-nationality groups in the completion of academic group work. The 2009 study in the UK followed the same methodology, collecting qualitative data from group interviews and focusing upon how student perceptions of working in diverse groups, particularly for assessment purposes, may have developed over the decade.

The data for the Montgomery (2009) study was drawn from teaching contexts focusing on Assessment for Learning (McDowell et al., 2005) or 'learning-oriented assessment', approaches which strongly emphasize the educational significance of peer support, peer assessment and the building of learning communities that include both students and staff. This approach encourages emphasis on the social and cultural contexts of learning, and aims, amongst other things, to enable students to build their own informal learning communities, again stemming from a belief that competences and effectiveness learned in doing this at university will equip them to make personal, professional and academic judgements in later life (Boud and Falchikov, 2006).

The study found that, in the particular contexts where peer exchange and other collaborative approaches were emphasized, attitudes to working in cross-cultural groups at university appeared more positive. Students appeared to be developing an awareness of the complexity of culture and beginning to perceive diversity within their own nationalities and within the nationalities of others. Students in the recent study viewed cross-cultural group work as part of their learning experience that was potentially preparing them for work in international contexts. In contrast to the Volet and Ang (1998) study, the sources of conflict in the groups were perceived for the most part to stem from sources other than cultural difference. Differences in academic discipline and variation in ideas about how to get things done were more prominent than culture, and where there were tensions these were seen to stem from inflexibility in these areas. There was also informality in relationships between students of different cultural backgrounds. In student talk about their cross-cultural interaction there were attempts to minimize the divides between cultures (Montgomery, 2009).

In contrast, studies carried out in more traditional teaching and learning contexts where group tasks were graded and thus 'high stakes' in nature (Carroll and Li, 2008) found evidence of negative student attitudes to intercultural group work. In their study the assessment task was not designed to value or draw upon the varied skills and experiences of the group, and all marks were based on the final product. This is distinct from the Assessment for Learning approaches in the environments focused on in the Montgomery (2009) study, where incremental tasks and 'low stakes' learning and assessment environments were emphasized. This suggests that the wider teaching, learning and assessment context could have an impact on student perceptions of intercultural learning. Further research in this area would be interesting.

Internationalization at home

Over the last decade a different approach to internationalizing the university experience has emerged and this has been termed 'internationalization at home' (IaH) (Teekens, 2000). IaH represents a significant shift in the way universities might view the drive to internationalize the research, teaching and services of Higher Education because it focuses not on the students who are already mobile, whom we currently call 'international students', but on the students and staff who are not. Internationalization at home is about promoting an international experience for all students and staff, but specifically for those who have not travelled beyond their own institution to new contexts (ibid.). The crucial aspect of this innovative approach to internationalization is that it does not focus on the international student group and attempt to work out how that 'problem' can somehow be 'fixed'. Instead, internationalization at home concentrates on the 'host' context and looks outwards, considering how the home campus context can become international and encourage all students and staff to view themselves as part of a global community in a global context that is interconnected.

Globalization, the force behind internationalized trade and commerce, has had a significant effect on the Higher Educational landscape, not least because students in many subject areas are bound for professional contexts that are now predominantly global in nature. Subject areas such as Business, Engineering, Computing and Design are discipline areas where students will be likely to need international outlooks and experiences in order to succeed. The principle of IaH is to provide that internationalized experience, not for the relatively small percentages of students who are able to travel abroad for placements or whole degrees, but for all students and staff who remain at home.

It is perhaps not a coincidence that the subject areas named above are those that have current concentrations in numbers of international students. The advantage of internationalization at home initiatives is that, in the course of IaH processes, it is likely that the internationally mobile students present in home institutions will become valuable sources of information and skills. The next section provides an example of a teaching, learning and research project that operates on the principle of internationalization at home.

The 'Global Studio': A case study

The Global Studio (GS) is a project based in the discipline of Design that promotes internationalization for all students and adheres to the principles of internationalization at home. The Global Studio is a Design course that is conducted across Higher Education contexts in England, Scotland and the Netherlands (Bohemia, Harman and Lauche, 2009) and more recently in Korea, Australia and the USA. Students in the participating institutions are given a Design brief to design a product to particular specifications. However, they are also required to design the product in conjunction with student partners in other national contexts and they work in groups, connected by virtual environments enabled by Web 2.0 technologies, on particular aspects of the design and production of a product for a particular international context and market (ibid.). The essential idea of the GS is to link student teams across the globe in 'client' and 'designer' roles. In this way students are equipped with 'specific knowledge and skills required to work in globally networked organisations and distributed design teams' (Bohemia, Harman and Lauche, 2009: 2).

The structure of the Global Studio is modelled on authentic design production and companies' processes in manufacturing products in the current globalized context. For example, modern design companies may be multinational corporations on different geographical sites and may need to operate in distributed settings where they are working with teams in a virtual environment. The Global Studio recreates this by asking student groups to work with each other across distance using ICTs, and, in recent iterations of the module, industry partners have also participated in the transnational collaborations. One of the rationales behind the GS was pragmatic, as the provision of opportunities to take part in international collaborations has previously been very expensive for institutions and students who have had to travel to international locations, meaning that opportunities to do so were limited. In short, the aim of the GS is to provide all students with experience of working in 'cross-disciplinary, cross-institutional, cross-cultural and geographically distributed design teams' (ibid., 2009: 18).

The implementation of the initial GS idea required students acting as designers to familiarize themselves with the local culture and practices of their client. This necessitated intercultural interaction that was based around and integrated with the academic task. It also required various stages of evaluation of the product design, one example being a kitchen timer, involving negotiation of cultural meaning that sometimes sparked linguistic and cultural misunderstandings. For example, students in the UK used the word 'cool' to describe an aspect of their product design, and this was interpreted by students in the Netherlands as the product needing 'some kind of cooling device to avoid overheating' rather than the intended meaning of 'cool' being 'trendy' (Bohemia, Harman and Lauche, 2009: 45). The process of discussion that unravelled that intercultural misunderstanding taught students about use of language and variation in cultural meanings across contexts, a useful understanding for future work in similar contexts.

Further case examples

The case example of the Global Studio is a large-scale project that required extensive organization to implement. However, other initiatives in a range of disciplines and on a smaller organizational scale are possible and happening. For example:

- Students working on designing 'ethical t-shirts' and experiencing work in a mock-up of an actual 'sweat-shop' where they produced the t-shirt in difficult conditions over an 8-hour production process. Detailed comparisons were made on aspects such as numbers of t-shirts made by students and workers in Bangladesh in the same time period (95 against 900 respectively). This activity developed awareness of conditions surrounding production processes in third world countries such as Bangladesh (Miller, 2009).
- Students on a Social Work course extending their research in Childhood Studies in a programme of work entitled 'Children's worlds', which explored, constructed and deconstructed children's experiences through an analysis of both local and world events. Students identified, located and developed a 'between country comparative analysis' of children's lives, impacted by poverty, war, health, and crime. Students produced posters and held a mini-conference, with two examples of work focusing on comparisons of attitudes to

mental health in the UK and Saudi Arabia and also a study of Child Poverty in India with comparisons to the UK (Brownrigg, 2009).

- Students on a Geography course exploiting their opportunities for international fieldwork to study the international and global implications of local and regional phenomena, including aspects such as climate change, ecosystem and habitat management, and sustainable food and water resources. International fieldwork enabled the students to gain first-hand, practical experience of such geographical issues in sometimes unfamiliar environments, situations and contexts (Mellor, 2009).
- Students on an Optoelectronics course taking part in annual seminars to exchange their work with partner institutions in France and Germany. The programme of workshops on various aspects of Optoelectronics rotates between the participating institutions and takes advantage of the complementary specialisms of the participating institutions in order to enhance the engineering education experience of students from each of the partner institutions. In addition, the programme aimed to provide students with an insight into the language and culture of each of the participating countries and enhance their interpersonal skills (Allen, 2009).

All of the above examples aim to link students with their global environment and encourage them to see their subject and themselves as part of an interconnected world.

Final comments

Despite the fact that ideas relating to internationalization and internationalization at home are developing rapidly, there appear to be very few examples of guidance for staff on approaches to teaching, learning and assessment practice that will support the development of intercultural skills in learning communities in Higher Education. There are scattered examples of guidance for practice on the development of intercultural competence. For example, Killick (2007) presents a series of case studies that capitalizes on opportunities for community engagement (international and home students working on projects in the community, such as student volunteering and local family support projects) as a means of students 'learning to live together across cultural boundaries whether national or local in nature' and thus a means of internationalizing the curriculum.

However, despite these pockets of good practice, there is little evidence of recommended overarching approaches that aim to promote international perspectives in staff and students. From a UK Higher Education context Spiro and Henderson (2007) acknowledge that the relationship between policy and practice is flawed and there is only

> a doubtful link between institutional Internationalisation of the Curriculum rhetoric and its impact on actual practice...As there is currently little knowledge about implementation of internationalisation...we have few foundations for valid, recognisable categories of good practice. (2007: 1)

Whilst there is a developing awareness of the approaches that might promote intercultural skills and competences, this idea is still associated solely with themes of internationalization and there has been little or no attempt to link current and innovative approaches to teaching, learning and assessment in general across universities with the principles inherent in moves to internationalize the curriculum. In short, the effective and inclusive strategies that are associated with the internationalization of the curriculum are effective approaches for teaching, learning and assessment strategies as a whole, and vice versa.

Internationalized university experiences cannot be easily met by simply increasing casual exposure between home and international students (Harrison, 2007). Rather, the tasks and activities that require students to engage in intercultural interaction should have meaning and authenticity in the students' personal and academic contexts.

If we are to move towards an understanding of what an international university experience entails, the intercultural Higher Education landscape should be presented not as a binary of international and home or self and other (Pierce, 2003) but as a complex site of struggle, tension and conflict. However, this 'troublesome space' in which intercultural interaction occurs should be seen not as being problematic but as useful and transformative (Savin-Baden, 2008). It may be that future research will show us that catalysts for these transformative troublesome spaces can be found in particular teaching, learning and assessment environments.

Postscript

To conclude this book a postscript is presented. Over the time that I have been writing this book I have kept in touch with several of the participants of the research, but in particular one student who is referred to in this book as 'Isken'. Since the time of the research presented here, Isken has completed his BA Honours, gained a scholarship for and completed an MA, and begun a PhD.

He has taken an active interest in the development of this book and has read drafts of chapters. He was very interested in reading comments he had made near the beginning of his education abroad and felt that it allowed him to reflect on how far he had come. He agreed to write a postscript to the book as himself rather than under the pseudonym he was given in the research. The postscript is his story. It is included here to illustrate the expectations, powerful motivations and personal, social and cultural context of one student.

Postscript

My name is Tshering Lama and I am from Nepal. I was one of the participants in the research that supports this book.

I really value the pages of this book that describe my experiences as they are a record of my early sense of hope combined with my sense of the challenges of being in a new learning environment. Today when I read those pages over and over again, I do feel proud of myself and how I have grown and progressed academically, socially and indeed professionally. After six years of being abroad I have still managed to keep two things that I mentioned in my interviews as strong as ever, maybe even growing stronger. These are my friends and my dream.

My social circle has certainly grown as I have moved forward but I still have very close relationships with the friends I mentioned during my interviews. My dream and goal of applying my education and knowledge for the benefit of my community back home in Nepal has certainly been challenging. But my current PhD research is starting to do this as it focuses on introducing Telemedicine (computer and phone contact with medical centres and hospitals) to remote environments in Nepal.

Reading the interviews in this book certainly helps me to appreciate my past and reminds me of my aims for the future. But my educational journey began well before my life at the university. My early childhood and early educational challenges still strongly influence who I am now.

However, the experience of being a student was (as documented in the research) and still is very exciting, challenging and enriching, though it can still sometimes be confusing!

My early life

I was born in a very remote village of Nepal in the mountains to the north east of Kathmandu. Perched 3,000 metres up in the Himalayas, my village is 70 miles from Kathmandu. It is a day's bus ride to the end of the road and then a 15 mile climb through some of the most beautiful trekking scenery in the region. It is a traditional mountain village with about 80 houses. The village has no power supply, lacks means of modern transport, proper communication and health facilities. Things which are taken for granted in the West.

I spent all my childhood in the village with my granny and four siblings. Due to economic hardship and lack of employment opportunities in the village at the time, many villagers moved to the cities of Nepal and India, so did my parents. My father travelled to Kathmandu and several parts of Nepal for his work. On many occasions my mother joined him so we children were left under the care and love of our grandmother.

Things changed when a village community school was opened in 1986 as without having to leave the village children could get an education. The school not only played a role in educational development but it equally contributed towards the village's economic and tourist developments. Volunteers started coming to the school in 1989 when it was in a small run-down building with 38 students and two teachers. It gradually became one of the best schools in the region. The school was rebuilt on a hilltop ridge, a short walk from the village, with 10 classrooms, a library, staff room and basic sports facilities. I attended the school from an early age and consider myself to be incredibly lucky to have been in the right place at the right time.

A student's life was not an easy one in the village due to other responsibilities we had to take on besides our school work. For example, I prepared food for all my siblings, helped my granny fetch water and had to feed the cattle (we had buffalos) and chickens before leaving for school. On many occasions, I collected firewood during my school lunch hour, and carried it home after school.

At the age of 11, I became Head Boy at the school and this gave me an early sense of responsibility. My responsibilities were conducting school assembly every morning, inspecting classes to make sure they were cleaned up by students, organizing events and attending meetings for the welfare of students. The skills I learnt were put to good use when organizing cultural exchange programmes and work festivals, or when chairing the Micro-credit system (a loan programme from the villagers to the villagers) in the village.

I became involved in health at the age of 13 as a volunteer health worker. In my spare time, I visited the sick, treated minor illnesses, learned to detect serious illnesses and refer them to city hospitals. Several volunteers joined me to help sick people in the village. While working as village health worker (known as a 'little doctor') I saw that people die of very common illnesses which could be prevented through basic public health programmes.

Leaving the village

I was one of the first group of students to graduate from the village school. The certificate was not only a School Leaving one but for me and for my friends, it was a Village Leaving certificate too. Saying goodbye to my birth place wasn't easy at all. This was the saddest time of my life up to then as I had to leave the school and the village but I dreamed of getting Higher Education qualifications. This was the start of many excitements and challenges. When I left I promised that I will never let my school and my village down whatever I do and wherever I go.

After completing school in the village, I moved to Kathmandu in search of further education and faced the greatest cultural shock ever in my life. Despite being reunited with parents and other friends who left school at the same time as me, I had so much difficulty in coping with city life. At the same time I was asking myself questions about Higher Education, which course should I take, where and how much will it cost my family. I had fears of bullying and discrimination and the list goes on. My parents were very supportive during that time and especially my brother, who had always been there for me.

I told my parents about my curiosity of doing 'A levels'. The curiosity certainly was influenced by volunteers from the UK as most of those who came to my village were recent A-level graduates, volunteering in their GAP year. In 1999 in Nepal, 'A levels' were new and taught only in a few schools mainly for children of elite families. However, my dad decided to take out a loan from the Agricultural Development Bank for my study (as Nepal still does not have loan facilities for education) and I was able to study A levels.

During and after taking my A levels, I became a volunteer at the only children's hospital in my country, providing care, medicine, blood and clothes for the sick and their families, and raising money to support them. In the year 2000, along with a few other friends from the village, we established a village Ex-Student Society in Kathmandu. We wanted to provide support and guidance for students seeking further studies, helping students in finding colleges and funds. I led the organization as a founding president from its establishment till 2002 and it later gained legal approval in 2003 as a non-government and not-for-profit organization.

University life in the UK since 2002

So with the generous help of one of the volunteers at my village school (and her family and other individuals who met me during my education in Nepal) I was provided with the finance I needed to come to the UK and was able to enrol for my BSc Health Development Course.

I graduated in 2005 with a BSc (Hons) Health Development Studies with an upper second class degree and continued on to a Master of Public Health at the same university. For my Master's I was awarded a new scholarship in recognition of my efforts in improving public health and the environment through volunteering.

My Master of Public Health became a turning point of my academic career. I focused all my assignments into health in developing countries. This certainly gave me a wider understanding of the health care situation in developing countries, mainly Nepal. Once I understood the challenges, I started looking into solutions. I looked at attempts made by individuals, organizations (both national and international) and government to overcome such challenges. Currently I am doing my PhD focusing on the possibilities and limitations of telemedicine (healthcare provided by modern communication) in rural Nepal.

Recently I was named the 'Regional International Student of the Year 2006'. I received an award and a commemoration trophy, attending a special reception with the British Prime Minister Tony Blair in recognition of my success. Besides this achievement, I was the subject of local newspaper articles and on local television. My interviews were broadcasted on TV channels and radio in Nepal. I was further honoured by our university establishing 20 scholarships for Nepalese students under my name 'Tshering Lama University Scholarships'. It was the greatest honour for me and for my country. Several students have now benefited from this scholarship.

Today, I am nearly halfway through my Doctorate programme. The PhD journey has certainly been very challenging but following my recent trips to Nepal, I have become more energized and optimistic about my own work and the possible utilization of my education. I hope I will find ways to work and save lives of people in the remote areas of my country. The enthusiasm, interest and willingness to support my work have been overwhelming and while this is an early phase of my research, I can clearly see myself developing Telemedicine in Nepal for many years to come.

Tshering Lama

Appendix 1 More Details of the Research Study

The research aimed to consider the social context of Higher Education through the perception of the international students themselves, and thus interview was chosen as a method to collect the views and interpretations of the students. In an attempt to widen these perceptions and include the reflective interpretations of the researcher herself, it was decided to support the interviews with an observation scheme. Shadowing was chosen as a means of approaching the observation.

Thus, a combination of semi-structured interviews and shadowing was chosen as the method through which to collect data. In keeping with the emergent approach to the research, it was decided to carry out a pilot study, the purpose of which was to collect a set of initial data that might inform the main part of the study. The pilot study also aimed to refine the methodology of the study itself. Indeed, this pilot study was an essential development in the study, as some significant changes in the methods were adopted following this first stage, and, as predicted, the pilot also raised some issues that were used to inform the main data collection phase.

To summarize, then, the study consists of data drawn from two focus groups: a pilot study involving four students and a main phase with seven students. Each student in the pilot and main phases was interviewed twice, each interview taking around one hour. Each student was also shadowed and observed for two separate days or a series of half-days and followed to lectures, seminars or tutorials and in their everyday movements around the campus. In addition to this, as a number of the participants were involved in the university Chess Club, some extra observation was carried out in this social context and a group discussion with members of the Chess Club was recorded. The interviews and Chess Club discussion were transcribed, and throughout the observation simultaneous field notes were made.

After the pilot study an initial analysis was carried out using the computer qualitative data analysis package 'Nudist 5', which enables an electronic, qualitative approach to coding of data. A series of codes were attributed to each section of the data and these codes (or free nodes) were given a structure that then informed the structure of the data presentation and analysis.

The table below shows a summary of the stages of the study and data collected.

Date	*Activity*	*Data collected*
March–April 2000	Focus groups carried out	2 × 2 hour focus groups recorded and notes made
December 2000–April 2001	Pilot study data collected	4 participants 4 interviews 4 observations
April 2002	Main data collection initiated	1 participant (Pei) 2 interviews and 2 formal observations
Jan–May 2003	Main data collection	6 participants 12 interviews (transcribed) 12 formal observations (recorded through field notes) Series of informal observations with Chess Club 1 Chess Club discussion (recorded and transcribed)

The interview schedule

The following questions were the basis for the semi-structured interviews. However, the interviews were informal in nature and in keeping with the philosophy of the research, where ideas or issues arose these were discussed with participants. In this sense some of the interview data was unstructured.

Why did you decide to come to study in the UK?

PROMPTS: (to be ticked or raised as appropriate)

- for qualifications
- to improve English?
- to meet British people?

Tell me about the people you know here in the UK?

PROMPTS: (to be ticked or raised as appropriate)

- how many people? who are they (e.g., students, staff?)
- UK or international?
- close friends or simple contacts?
- do they live near you?
- how do you know them?
- how often do you see them?
- why do you contact them/or they you? (e.g., social, academic, advice, information?)
- do your friends know each other?

Do the people you know help/support you? How?

PROMPTS: (to be ticked or raised as appropriate)

- emotionally?
- with information?
- on your course?
- with practical advice on living in the UK?
- with getting used to differences in culture in the UK?

Do you help/support the people you know? How?

PROMPTS: (to be ticked or raised as appropriate)

- emotionally?
- with information?
- on their course?
- with practical advice on living in the UK?
- with getting used to differences in culture in the UK?

Who do you talk to if you feel upset or depressed?

PROMPTS: (to be ticked or raised as appropriate)

- how or where do you contact them?

Do you feel that you have good/successful relationships with people around you in the UK?

PROMPTS: (to be ticked or raised as appropriate)

- people on your course?
- people around the university?
- people in the community outside the university?
- in what way are the relationships 'successful'?

Do you have frequent contact with friends and family back at home in your own country?

PROMPTS: (to be ticked or raised as appropriate)

- with family?
- with friends?
- how often?
- why do you contact them? (e.g., for information, for emotional support, to chat?)
- how does this help/hinder?

Do you feel that you are successful/doing well on your course?

PROMPTS: (to be ticked or raised as appropriate)

- academically?
- socially?
- are you doing the best you could do? Why or why not?

What helps you to carry on with your course and be successful?

PROMPTS: (to be ticked or raised as appropriate)

- your friends/people you know?
- what do they do or say that helps?

Do you think that the people you have around you here in the UK help you to be successful on your course?

PROMPTS: (to be ticked or raised as appropriate)

- how do they do this?

Appendix 2
A Reflective Account of the Researcher

In this appendix I will present a profile of myself as the researcher. I reflect on my personal life before the study began as a means of placing the study in context. The appendix also explains how I came to start this research, considering my early views of the research and reflecting on my expectations of how the study would turn out. Following this I consider how my views have changed over the course of the study and how my changing views have become part of the research itself.

When I was a child my parents took me on holidays to Europe, often to France and Italy. These trips interested me in travel, and as a young adult I went to live abroad in France and then Turkey and was away for four years. I taught English and learned the languages of the countries where I lived. I developed a strong interest in understanding and getting to know the culture and people of these countries. I also experienced at first hand what it means to live and work in another country, and experienced the challenges and advantages of the first stages of being in a new environment. My personal experiences had initiated an interest in what it means to leave your home country and live abroad, living in an unfamiliar linguistic and social environment. On my return to the UK I began work in Higher Education as a Lecturer in English Language to international students and was offered a full-time post at a university in the south of the UK.

After five years teaching international students I began work at a 'new' university in the north of England as International Student Adviser. The post entailed providing practical advice and support for the international students coming to the university. Students came to discuss their difficulties with me and I tried to advise them and provide information to help their transition from their home countries into the university and the local community. Many of the issues raised by students related to their unfamiliarity with the sometimes inflexible administrative and organizational systems of the university and difficulty in interacting with the community at large. At the same time, there were many examples of difficulties with understanding and getting to know people. Students talked to me about their feelings of isolation, particularly socially, and the difficulty of meeting and talking to home students and people in the wider community of the university and beyond. The experience of listening to students talking about these topics, coupled with my personal experiences as described above, led to my interest in beginning an empirical study into the nature of the international student's social and personal experience.

When I first began to formulate a research proposal I already had some fairly definite views on what I expected to find. The most interesting aspect of reflecting on those set views is that I can now see how my strong belief in the 'truth' of those views evaporated over the course of the study. I supposed at that time that all international students were socially isolated and had few or no links to a social life in the UK. I had a rather narrow view, which may have been a result of the nature of the job I had been doing. Students mainly came to see me to share problems or difficulties, and this had provided me with a rather limited view of the nature of their experiences as a whole. As I began to learn more about research methods, and as I began to collect data for the study, my perceptions began to change. As I talked to the students in depth and followed them in their everyday lives, I began to see a picture of students who were more confident and independent than I had at first supposed. They were focused and highly motivated, with strong support networks within their own nationality and other nationality groups. The original view I had of these students was that they were not linked into a strong group and that they lacked a strong focus. After carrying out some of the research I found that their relationships with UK students were, on the whole, superficial, but there were relationships there and I had expected none.

It was at this early stage that I decided that I wanted to approach the research in a different way from that I had at first planned. My first thought was to have a fairly strong hypothesis that I would test against the data, but as I began the first stages of the research I realized that many of my preconceptions about what I would find were being contradicted. It was at this early stage that I decided to follow a more emergent approach and to combine this with a reflective stance that acknowledged my own part in making and constructing the outcomes and text of the research. I chose this more reflective approach because one of its aims is to 'try to stimulate critical reflection and awareness' (Alvesson and Skoldberg, 2000: 6). It is hoped that the reflective element in the responses of the students will provide readers themselves with an opportunity to reflect on the issues being raised, with a view to becoming more aware of the significance of the context being described. I hope that this research will have the same effect on the reader that it had on me as the researcher: the effect of developing a broader and more critical awareness and understanding of the social context of the travelling student.

References

Adams, R. G. and G. Allan (1998). *Placing Friendship in Context.* Cambridge: Cambridge University Press.

Allen, J. (2009). Developing international perspectives through Opto-electronics. Conference paper at *Building an International Community: How Assessment for Learning Can Help.* Northumbria University, January.

Altheide, D. L. and J. M. Johnson (1994). Criteria for assessing interpretive validity in qualitative research. In Denzin, N. K. and Y. S. Lincoln (eds). *Handbook of Qualitative Research* (1st edition). London: Sage.

Alvesson, M. and K. Skoldberg (2000). *Reflexive Methodology: New Vistas for Qualitative Research.* London: Sage.

Ball, S., M. Maguire and S. Macrae (2000). *Choice Pathways and Transition Post-16.* London: Routledge.

Barrett, R. and J. Malcolm (2006). Embedding plagiarism education in the assessment process. *International Journal for Educational Integrity* 2(1): 38–45.

Baumann, G. (1996). *Contesting Culture: Discourses of Identity in Multi-Ethnic London.* Cambridge: Cambridge University Press.

Beard, C., S. Clegg and K. Smith (2007). Acknowledging the affective in Higher Education. *British Educational Research Association* 33(2): 235–252.

Beaver, B. and B. Tuck (1998). The adjustment of overseas students at a tertiary institution in New Zealand. *New Zealand Journal of Educational Studies* 33(2): 167–180.

Belcher, J. (1995). Thinking globally, acting locally: Strategies for universities. *Journal of International Education* 7(6/3): 5–13.

Bhabha, H. (1994). *The Location of Culture.* London: Routledge.

Biggs, J. (1999). *Teaching for Quality Learning at University*. Buckingham: SRHE.

Bochner, S., B. M. McLeod and A. Lin (1977). Friendship patterns of overseas students: A functional model. *International Journal of Psychology* 12(4): 277–294.

Bohemia, E., K. Harman and K. Lauche (2009). *The Global Studio.* Amsterdam: IOS Press BV.

Bond, M. H., V. Zegarac and H. Spencer-Oatey (2000). Culture as an explanatory variable: Problems and possibilities. In Spencer-Oatey, H. (ed.). *Culturally Speaking: Managing Rapport through Talk Across Cultures.* London: Continuum.

Bonvillain, N. (2003). *Language, Culture, and Communication: The Meaning of Messages* (4th edition). New Jersey: Prentice Hall.

Boud, D. and N. Falchikov (2006). Aligning assessment with long-term learning. *Assessment and Evaluation in Higher Education* 31(4): 399–413. Bourdieu, P. (1985). *The Forms of Capital.* New York: Greenwood.

Brownrigg, A. (2009). Developing an international perspective on Childhood Studies. Conference paper at *Building an International Community: How Assessment for Learning Can Help*. Northumbria University, January.

Bruch, T. and A. Barty (1998). Internationalising British students and institutions. In Scott, P. (ed.). *The Globalization of Higher Education.* Buckingham: SRHE and Open University Press.

Byram, M. (1998). *Teaching and Assessing Intercultural Communicative Competence.* Clevedon: Multilingual Matters.

Byram, M. and A. Feng (2004). Culture and language learning: Teaching, research and scholarship. *Language Teaching* 37: 149–168.

Byram, M. and M. Fleming (1998). *Language Learning in Intercultural Perspective.* Cambridge: Cambridge University Press.

Caglar, A. (2006). Transdisciplinarity and transnationalism: Challenges to Internationalisation at Home. In Teekens, H. (ed). *Internationalisation at Home: A global perspective.* The Hague: Nuffic.

Callan, H. (1998). Internationalisation in Europe. In Scott, P. (ed.). *The Globalization of Higher Education.* Buckingham: SRHE and Open University Press.

Carroll, J. and R. Li (2008). Assessed group work in culturally diverse groups: Is normative guidance useful in addressing students' worries about grades? Conference paper presented at *Oxford Brookes University: Using informal and formal curricula to improve interaction between international and home students.* June.

Carroll, J. and J. Ryan (2005). *Teaching International Students: Improving Learning for All.* Oxford: Routledge.

Caruana, V. (2006). The internationalisation of UK Higher Education: A review of selected material. Higher Education Academy. Available at http://www.heacademy.ac.uk/assets/york/documents/ourwork/tla/internationalisation/lit_review_internationalisation_of_uk_he_v2.pdf (last accessed 16 March 2008).

Chomsky, N. (1965). *Aspects of the Theory of Syntax.* Cambridge, MA: MIT Press.

Clifford, V. (2009). Editorial: Using formal and informal curricula to improve interactions between home and international students. *Journal of Studies in International Education* 13(2): 203–204.

Coleman, J. (2000). *Social Capital in the Creation of Human Capital.* Woburn, MA: Butterworth-Heinemann.

Cortazzi, M. and L. Jin (2006). Changing practices in Chinese Cultures of Learning. *Language, Culture and Curriculum* 19(1): 15–20.

Davies, J. and K. Ecclestone (2008). 'Straightjacket' or 'springboard for sustainable learning'? The implications of formative assessment practices in vocational learning cultures. *Curriculum Journal* 19(2): 71–86.

Deardorff, D. K. (2006). Identification and assessment of intercultural competence as a student outcome of internationalisation. *Journal of Studies in International Education* 10(3): 241–266.

De Vita, G. (2001). Learning styles, culture and inclusive instruction in the multicultural classroom: A business and management perspective. *Innovations in Education and Teaching International* 38(2): 165–174.

De Wit, H. (1999). Changing rationales for the internationalisation of Higher Education. *International Higher Education* 15: 2–3.

De Wit, H. (2002). *Internationalisation of Higher Education in the United States of America and Europe: A Historical, Comparative, and Conceptual Analysis*. Westport, CT: Greenwood Press.

Dixon, M. (2006). Globalisation and International Higher Education: Contested positionings. *Journal of Studies in International Education* 10: 319–333.

Duranti, A. (1997). *Linguistic Anthropology.* Cambridge: Cambridge University Press.

Durrell, L. (1957). *Justine.* New York: Dutton.

Edwards, J. (1995). *Multilingualism.* London: Penguin.

Edwards, J. (2007). Challenges and opportunities for the internationalisation of higher education in the coming decade: Planned and opportunistic initiatives in American institutions. *Journal of Studies in International Education* 11(3/4): 373–381.

Erikson, E. (1959). *Identity and the Lifecycle: Psychological Issues*. New York: International Universities Press.

Finkbeiner, C. (2005). Constructing third space together: The principles of reciprocity and cooperation. *Interrogating Third Spaces in Language Teaching, Learning and Use Conference.* CETEAL, Leicester University, 27 June.

Fok, W. P. (2007). Internationalisation of Higher Education in Hong Kong. *International Education Journal* 8(1): 184–193.

Francis, B. and L. Archer (2005). British-Chinese pupils' and parents' constructions of the value of education. *British Educational Research Journal* 31(1): 89–108.

Furnham, A. (1997). *Being an Overseas student.* London: Routledge.

Fukuyama, F. (1999). *Social Capital and Civil Society.* Institute of Public Policy, George Mason University. IMF Conference on Second Generation reforms. Available at http://imf.org/external/pubs/ft/seminar/1999/reforms/fukuyama.htm#I (last accessed 18 March 2008).

Gannon-Leary, P. and J. Smailes (2004). Diverse student needs: The challenge of teaching international students. *LTRN-BEST conference. Reflection on Teaching: The Impact on Learning.* Edinburgh.

Geertz, C. (1973). *The Interpretation of Cultures.* New York: Basic.

Gunn, S. (2005). Introduction. In Cullingford, C. and S. Gunn (eds). *Globalisation, Education and Culture Shock.* Aldershot, UK: Ashgate.

Haggis, T. (2003). Constructing images of ourselves? A critical investigation into 'approaches to learning' Research in Higher Education. *British Educational Research Journal* 29(1): 89–104.

Haigh, M. (2008). Internationalisation, planetary citizenship and Higher Education Inc. *Compare: A Journal of Comparative Education* 38(4): 427–440.

Hall, E. T. (1998). Gifts of wisdom: An interview with E. T. Hall. *The E-Journal of Intercultural Relations* 1 Summer (3).

Harrison, N. (2007). Internationalisation at home, mindfulness and passive xenophobia: Using *Integrated Threat Theory* to explore the intercultural discourse between domestic and international Higher Education students in the United Kingdom. Conference paper. *Annual Conference of the Society for Research into Higher Education (SRHE).* December.

Harrison, N. and N. Peacock (2007). Understanding the UK student response to internationalisation. *UKCOSA Worldviews* Summer.

Ho, E., P. Holmes and J. Cooper (2004). *Review and Evaluation of International Literature on Managing Cultural Diversity in the Classroom*. Report prepared for the Ministry of Education, New Zealand. University of Waikato, NZ.

Hodkinson, P., H. Colley and J. Malcolm (2003). The interrelationship between informal and formal learning. *Journal of Workplace Learning* 15(7/8): 313–318.

Hofstede, G. (1984). *Culture's Consequences.* London: Sage.

Holliday, A. (1999). Small cultures. *Applied Linguistics* 20(2): 237–264.

Holliday, A. (2007a). The persistence of constructions of superiority and inferiority in cultural description. Unpublished paper, Department of English and Language Studies, Canterbury Christ Church University.

Holliday, A. (2007b). Interrogating the concept of stereotypes in intercultural communication. Unpublished paper, Department of English and Language Studies, Canterbury Christ Church University.

Holliday, A., M. Hyde and J. Kullman (2004). *Intercultural Communication: An Advanced Resource Book*. Abingdon, Oxon: Routledge.

Hollway, W. and T. Jefferson (2000). *Doing Qualitative Research Differently.* London: Sage.

Hymes, D. (1972). On communicative competence. In Pride, J. B. and J. Holmes (eds). *Sociolinguistics*. Harmondsworth: Penguin.

Iredale, R. (1994). The power from change. *Journal of International Education* 5(1): 7–19.

I-Graduate, International student insight (2005). *International Student Barometer.* IGI Services Limited.

Jackson, C. (2003). Transformation into higher education: Engendered implications for academic self-concept. *Oxford Review of Education* 29(3): 331–346.

Jackson, J. (2008). *Language, Identity and Study Abroad: Sociocultural Perspectives*. London: Equinox.

Killick, D. (2007). Internationalisation and engagement with the wider community. In Jones, E. and S. Brown (eds). *Internationalising Higher Education*. Abingdon, Oxon: Routledge.

Kinnell, M. (1990). *The Learning Experiences of Overseas Students.* Buckingham: SRHE.

Kishun, R. (1998). Internationalisation in South Africa. In Scott, P. (ed.). *The Globalisation of Higher Education.* Buckingham: SRHE and Open University.

Knight, J. (1995). What does Internationalisation really mean? *UKCOSA Journal* January: 5–9.

Knight, J. (1997). Internationalisation of Higher Education: A conceptual framework. In Knight, J. and H. De Wit (eds). *Internationalisation of Higher Education in Asia Pacific Countries.* Amsterdam: European Association for International Education.

Knight, J. and H. De Wit (1997). *Internationalisation of Higher Education in Asia Pacific Countries.* Amsterdam: European Association for International Education.

Kramsch, C. (1998). The privilege of the intercultural speaker. In Byram, M. and M. Fleming. *Language Learning in Intercultural Perspective.* Cambridge: Cambridge University Press.

Kramsch, C. (2006). The Multilingual Subject. *International Journal of Applied Linguistics* 16(1): 97–110.

Kristeva, J. (1991). *Strangers to Ourselves.* New York: Columbia University Press.

Kroeber, A. L. and C. Kluckhohn (1952). *Culture: A Critical Review of Concepts and Definitions.* Cambridge, MA: Peabody Museum.

Lave, J. and E. Wenger (1991). *Situated Learning: Legitimate Peripheral Participation.* Cambridge: Cambridge University Press.

Leask, B. (2004). Plagiarism and cultural diversity: Responsibilities, accountabilities and pedagogy. *Plagiarism: Prevention, Practice and Policy Conference*, Northumbria University, 28–30 June.

Leask, B. (2009). Using formal and informal curricula to improve interactions between home and international students. *Journal of Studies in International Education* 13(2): 205–221.

Lechte, J. (1994). *Fifty Key Contemporary Thinkers: From Structuralism to Postmodernity.* London: Routledge.

Lee, J. J. and C. Rice (2007). Welcome to America? International student perceptions of discrimination. *Higher Education* 53: 381–409.

Leonard, D., C. Pelletier and L. Morley (2004). *The Experiences of International Students in UK Higher Education: A Review of Unpublished Material.* London: UKCOSA.

Lincoln, Y. and E. Guba (1985). *Naturalistic Enquiry.* Newbury Park, CA: Sage.

McDonald, S. (2005). Studying actions in context. *Qualitative Research* 5(4): 455–473.

McDowell, L., K. Sambell, V. Bazin, R. Penlington, D. Wakelin, H. Wickes and J. Smailes (2005). Assessment for learning: Current practice exemplars from the Centre for Excellence in Teaching and Learning. *Northumbria University Red Guide*, Paper 22.

McLean, P. and L. Ransom (2005). Building intercultural competencies: Implications for academic skills development. In Carroll, J. and J. Ryan (eds). *Teaching International Students: Improving Learning for All.* Oxford: Routledge.

Mann, S. J. (2001). Alternative perspectives on the student experience: Alienation and engagement. *Studies in Higher Education* 26(1): 7–19.

Marton, F., D. Hounsell and N. Entwistle (1997). *The Experience of Learning: Implications for Teaching and Studying in Higher Education*. Edinburgh: Scottish Academic Press.

Marton, F. and K. Trigwell (2000). Variato est mater studorium. *Higher Education Research and Development* 19: 381–395.

Mellor, T. (2009). The experience of overseas fieldwork in Geography. Conference paper at *Building an international community: How assessment for learning can help*. Northumbria University, January 2009.

Merrick, B. (2004). *Broadening Our Horizons: International Students in UK Universities and colleges*. London: UKCOSA.

Miller, D. (2009). Internationalising the curriculum with ethical fashion. Conference paper at *Building an international community: How assessment for learning can help*. Northumbria University, January.

Mills, S. (2000). *Youth Lifestyles in a Changing World*. Buckingham: Open University Press.

Milroy, L. and M. Gordon (2003). *Sociolinguistics: Method and Interpretation*. Oxford: Blackwell.

Montgomery, C. (2009). A decade of internationalisation: Has it influenced students' views of cross-cultural group work at university? *Journal of Studies in International Education* 13(2): 256–270.

Nippert-Eng, C. (1995). *Home and Work. Negotiating Boundaries through Everyday Life*. Chicago, IL: University of Chicago Press.

Oxford, R. and N. Anderson (1995). A cross-cultural view of learning styles. *Language Teaching* 28: 201–215.

Peacock, N. and N. Harrison (2009). 'It's so much easier to go with what's easy': 'Mindfulness' and the discourse between home and international students in the UK. *Journal of Studies in International Education*. Available online at http://jsi.sagepub.com/cgi/content/abstract/1028315308319508v1 (last accessed April 2009).

Pelletier, C. (2003). *The Experiences of International Students in UK Higher Education: A review of Unpublished Research*. London: UKCOSA.

Pierce, A. (2003). What Does It Mean to Live In-between? Paper presented at the 4th annual IALIC conference, Lancaster University, 16 December.

Pilisuk, M. and S. Hillier Parks (1986). *The Healing Web: Social Networks and Human Survival*. USA: University Press of New England.

Prosser, M. and K. Trigwell (1999). *Understanding Teaching and Learning*. Buckingham: SRHE and Open University Press.

Richards, J., J. Platt and H. Weber (1985). *Longman Dictionary of Applied Linguistics*. Essex: Longman.

Roberts, C. and S. Sarangi (1993). 'Culture' revisited in intercultural communication. In Boswood, T., R. Hoffman and P. Tung (eds). *Perspectives on English for International Communication.* Hong Kong: Hong Kong City Polytechnic, 97–102.

Ryan, J. and K. Louie (2007). 'False Dichotomy?' 'Western' and 'Confucian' concepts of scholarship and learning. *Educational Philosophy and Theory* 39(4): 404–417.

Savin-Baden, M. (2008). *Learning Spaces: Creating Opportunities for Knowledge Creation in Academic Life.* Maidenhead: OUP.

Schwandt, T. A. (1994). Constructivist, interpretivist approaches to human inquiry. In Denzin, N. K. and Y. S. Lincoln (eds). *Handbook of Qualitative Research* (1st edition). London: Sage.

Scott, P. (ed.) (1998). *The Globalization of Higher Education.* Buckingham: SRHE and Open University Press.

Shipton, A. (2005). *Being and Becoming a Student in HE: An Appreciation of an Evolving Sense of Self.* Unpublished MPhil Thesis, College of York St John.

Shirato, T. and S. Yell (2000). *Communication and Culture.* London: Sage.

Smith, M. (2000). *Culture: Reinventing The social Sciences.* Buckingham: Open University Press.

Spencer-Oatey, H. (2000). *Culturally Speaking: Managing Rapport through Talk Across Cultures.* London: Continuum.

Spiro, J. and J. Henderson (2007). Internationalising the curriculum at Brookes: A student perspective. Presented at the Brookes Student Learning Experience Conference, May.

Spurling, N. (2006). The experience of international students. The internationalisation of UK Higher Education: a review of selected material. *Higher Education Academy.* Available at http://www.heacademy.ac.uk/assets/york/documents/ourwork/tla/internationalisation/lit_review_internationalisation_of_uk_he_v2.pdf (last accessed 16 March 2008).

Stone, N. (2006). Conceptualising intercultural effectiveness for university teaching. *Journal of Studies in International Education* 10: 334–356.

Strauss, A. and J. Corbin (1994). Grounded theory methodology: An Overview. In Denzin, N. K. and Y. S. Lincoln (eds). *Handbook of Qualitative Research.* London: Sage.

Sysoyev, P. V. (2002). *Identity, Culture, and Language Teaching.* The University of Iowa: Center for Russian, East European, and Eurasian Studies.

Tanaka, J., H. Spencer-Oatey and T. Cray (2000). It's not my fault!: Japanese and English responses to unfounded accusations. In Spencer-Oatey, H (ed.). *Culturally Speaking: Managing Rapport through Talk Across Cultures.* London: Continuum.

Tang, C. (1994). *Assessment and Student Learning: Effects of Modes of Assessment on Students' Preparation Strategies.* Oxford, UK: The Oxford Centre for Staff Development, Oxford Brookes University.

Teekens, H. (2000). Teaching and learning in the international classroom. In Crowther, P., M. Joris, M. Otten, B. Nilsson, H. Teekens and B. Wachter (eds). *Internationalisation at Home: A Position Paper*. Sweden: European Association for International Education.

Teekens, H. (2006). Internationalisation at home: A background paper. In Teekens, H. (ed.). *Internationalisation at Home: A Global Perspective*. The Hague: Nuffic.

Teichler, U. (2004). The changing debate on internationalisation of higher education. *Higher Education* 48: 5–26.

Toffler, A. (1990). *Powershift: Knowledge, Wealth and Violence at the edge of the 21st Century.* New York: Bantam.

Trahar, S. (2004). *A Part of the Landscape: Experiences of Being a Practitioner Researcher in an International higher education community*. SRHE Conference, 14 December. Graduate School of Education, University of Bristol, HOME.

Trahar, S. (2007). *Teaching and Learning: The International Higher Education Landscape.* Bristol: Escalate, The Higher Education Academy Education Subject Centre.

Trahar, S. (2008). Close encounters of the cultural kind: Reflections of a practitioner researcher in a UK Higher Education context. In Hellsten, M. and A. Reid (eds). *Researching International Pedagogies: Sustainable Practice for Teaching and Learning in Higher Education*. Australia: Springer.

Trouillot, M. R. (2003). *Global Transformations; Anthropology and the Modern World.* New York: Palgrave Macmillan.

Turner, Y. (2006). Students from mainland China and critical thinking in PG Business and management degrees: Teasing out tensions of culture, style and substance. *International Journal of Management Education* 5: 3–11.

Ullman, C. (1998). *Social Identity and the Adult ESL Classroom.* ERIC Digest, 19 February. Available at http://www.ericdigests.org/1998–2/social.htm (last accessed 14 February 2006).

Unterhalter, E. and D. Green (1997). *Making the Adjustment: Orientation Programmes for International Students*. London: UKCOSA.

Vandermensbrugghe, J. (2004). The unbearable vagueness of critical thinking in the context of the Anglo-Saxonisation of Education. *International Education Journal* 5(3): 417–422.

Volet, S. E. and G. Ang (1998). Culturally mixed groups on International Campuses: An opportunity for inter-cultural learning. *Higher Education Research and Development* 17(1): 5–23.

Wachter, B. (1999). *Internationalisation in Higher Education.* Bonn: Lemmens Verlags & Mediengesellschaft.

Walker, M., S. Wasserman and B. S. Wellman (1994). *Statistical Models for Social Support Networks.* London: Sage.

Wenger, E. (1998). *Communities of Practice: Learning, Meaning and Identity.* Cambridge University Press.

Wenger, E., R. McDermott and W. Snyder (2002). *Cultivating Communities of Practice: A Guide to Managing Knowledge.* Boston, MA: Harvard Business School Press.

Williams, R. (1983). *Keywords.* London: Fontana.

Ylanne-McEwan, V. and N. Coupland (2000). Accommodation theory: A conceptual resource for intercultural sociolinguistics. In Spencer-Oatey, H. (ed.). *Culturally Speaking: Managing Rapport through Talk Across Cultures.* London: Continuum.

Index